STACK YOUR SAVINGS

HOW TO SAVE MORE MONEY, SLASH YOUR SPENDING, AND MASTER YOUR FINANCES

S.J. SCOTT
REBECCA LIVERMORE

DISCLAIMER

Contents

INTRODUCTION

"Money doesn't grow on trees!"

Perhaps your parents spoke such words to you when you were growing up. As a teenager, you may have rolled your eyes in response, but once you got out on your own, the saying made more sense.

While it's true this saying reveals a scarcity mindset, the fact of the matter is: in the real world, many of us struggle with earning and saving money. Often, it doesn't even matter *how much money* you make—we all have unique challenges when it comes to money.

For instance, perhaps you can relate to one or more of the following scenarios:

You Work at a Low-Paying Job

People fall into the low-income category for many reasons. Perhaps you're a student or a recent graduate who hasn't yet landed a good job.

Maybe you're a single parent. Or you might be a one-income family, with one parent staying home to take care of the kids. Not only is money tight, but as a stay-at-home parent, you wish you had a way to contribute to your family's financial well-being.

Perhaps you're a retiree, and you haven't saved enough for retirement. At this stage in your life, you don't want to work or perhaps can't find work or are physically unable to work. Yet your pension doesn't cover your living expenses, much less the things you'd love to do such as travel.

Maybe you've lost your job or are underemployed and now struggle to make your house or car payment.

Regardless of which scenario fits you, the bottom line is that your income isn't enough to meet your expenses.

You Make Decent Money but Have High Expenses

Perhaps you have an average, or even sizeable income, but you have big expenses.

Maybe for good or bad reasons, you've racked up a lot of debt. Perhaps you, your spouse, or your child has medical issues that resulted in thousands upon thousands of dollars in medical bills. Perhaps you live in a city like San Francisco or New York that has a very high cost of living, where your mortgage—even on a fairly modest home—eats up half your income.

Regardless of the reason, no matter how hard you work, at the end of the month you have little money left.

You Struggle with Planning for the Future

Maybe you're not struggling to pay your day-to-day bills, but you don't have much, if any, money left over to save for retirement, toward a down payment on a home, or for your children's college education.

You may feel hopeless when you think of the future because it just doesn't seem possible to make progress in those areas.

You Want to Afford the Finer Things in Life

Perhaps you're one of the fortunate ones who has enough income to pay your bills and invest in your retirement, but there's not much left for the finer things in life. You haven't gone on a real vacation in years. You can only dream about having nice furniture, a newer car, or name-brand clothing for yourself or your children.

Granted, these things aren't necessary for a happy life, and some may even scoff at your desire for the finer things in life. But when it comes right down to it, there's nothing wrong with going on a dream vacation, buying designer clothing, or sending your kids to an exclusive private school.

Unfortunately, if you're like many people, in spite of having a good job, up to this point, you can only dream about such luxuries.

You Dream of Early Retirement

Perhaps you dream of early retirement or want to reach a point of financial independence where you can live off the interest of your savings. As we'll explain, this is a goal Steve is currently working on.

You may not mind working, but you don't want to *have to* work, or you may hope to get to the point where you can afford to do more meaningful work, even if it pays less.

The bottom line?

It doesn't matter what financial goal you're striving for. The answer to each of these scenarios is to is build the "stack your savings" habit.

Introducing *Stack Your Savings*

In the following book, *Stack Your Savings: How to Save More Money, Slash Your Spending, and Master Your Finances*, we will talk about the power of making small financial decisions that will have a positive, cumulative effect on your financial situation. Each action might not *seem* important, but if you apply this strategy for over a period of months—even years—you'll end up saving a lot of money.

Many people make the mistake of thinking that all their problems will be solved if they simply make more money. Increasing income may help, and it's something that especially those in the low-income category may want to work on, but it's only one part of the equation.

The other part of the equation is **saving money**. In fact, saving money is often preferable to making more money.

Consider this: You pay taxes on the money you make, but not the money you save. So any savings you can find will have a larger impact on your personal finances than making more money.

For example, if you make $1,000 and pay 20% in taxes, you actually end up with $800. But if you save $1,000 by getting good deals, that's worth the full $1,000. In addition to that, increasing your income can put you into a higher tax bracket, which compounds this problem. Because of this, if you have a choice between reducing your monthly expenses by $1,000 and making an extra $1,000, reducing costs makes more sense.

In addition to paying fewer taxes, here are a few other benefits to consider.

Benefit 1: You Spend Less on Necessities

If you spend less on necessities, you'll have more money to pay down debt, which will ultimately lead to reducing your overall monthly expenses.

Even without debt, reducing your expenditures on necessities such as housing, transportation, and food gives you more money to plan for the future in the form of things like saving for retirement, adding to your child's 529 college savings fund, and saving for a down payment on a home.

Benefit 2: You Enjoy Luxuries You Otherwise Couldn't Afford

Do you dream of things that seem beyond your reach? Whether big or small, learning to save money can make those dreams reality.

For example, Steve's wife, Kristin, is a genius when it comes to finding "like-new" clothes for their son. None of these items are purchased directly from stores. Instead, Kristin has a system where she buys "bags of clothes" from the wealthier neighborhoods in their area. And the best part? Many of these items were never worn—some still even have the tag on them.

Rebecca took a dream vacation to China, thanks to her step-dad, who came across an advertisement for an all-inclusive two-week tour package for a measly $1,000.

Not only did this low-cost fee cover airfare from the United States and travel within country, it also included all meals, shows, and everything else she could possibly want or need. More importantly, it provided her with the opportunity to go on a trip with her step-dad, who has since passed away, and her mother, who is now old enough that such a trip would likely be too demanding. It's something that would have been unaffordable had it not been for the great deal.

Benefit 3: You Create More Freedom in Your Life

Learning to live on less also gives you freedom. For instance, it can give you freedom to transition from a job you hate to a job you love that pays less. It also positions you to be okay financially in case of a job loss.

For instance, Rebecca and her husband bought a home that was half of their prequalified amount. The relatively low house payment made it easier on them when her husband lost his job and also made it possible for Rebecca to eventually quit her job and write full-time.

Steve, on the other hand, is primarily focusing on early retirement, so every penny he saves will help him achieve this long-term goal.

Regardless of how financial freedom looks to you, saving money will help you get there.

Why Should YOU Focus on Saving Money?

The goals we've mentioned so far—retiring early, adding to retirement accounts, and going on dream vacations—matter. The problem is that goals without execution won't go anywhere. That's why you need habits to turn these goals into an action plan.

We define the stack your savings habit as a mix of one-time

actions with daily, weekly, and monthly habits that help you stay on track and make consistent progress toward your goals. While we include a treasure trove of ideas in this book, it's up to you to turn this information into action.

Put simply: Whenever you discover a concept that will help you save money, your job will be to build it as a permanent habit. But don't worry—we have an entire section dedicated to showing you how to take the information in this book and turn it into a simple action plan.

Saving in Cycles

According to a study[1] done by Leona Tam and Utpal Dholakia, those who think of savings in cyclical terms are estimated to save 74% more than those who think of money linearly.

Thinking of money linearly views life in past, present, and future terms. People with this mindset often have an optimistic view of the future and, therefore, think they'll be able to save more in the future. As a result, they don't worry about saving much now.

For instance, they may think, *When my kids are grown, I'll be able to save more toward retirement.* They then justify not saving toward retirement now. Unfortunately, the future isn't always as rosy as one might hope, and because of it, people with this mindset may not ever get around to saving.

In contrast, cyclical savings focuses on repetition (what we refer to as habits) now, rather than putting things off for a "better" time. As you develop the money saving habit, not only will you

---

1   http://ro.uow.edu.au/cgi/viewcontent.cgi?article=1317&context=buspapers

save more now, you'll also naturally save more in the future with minimal effort.

For example, if you create the habit of investing a set percentage, such as 15% out of every paycheck, you'll automatically invest more as your income increases.

The bottom line is that now is the time to learn to save money on the big things and then apply that savings toward your big-picture financial goals.

Regardless of your current financial situation, there's no time like the present to develop the stack your savings habit!

About the Authors

Stack Your Savings is a collaboration between two authors, Rebecca Livermore and Steve "S.J." Scott.

Rebecca is a naturally frugal person. She even once ended up on the local news for her grocery shopping skills. At the time, she was a stay-at-home mom, and one of her greatest financial contributions was feeding her family on a dime—literally. She scoured the newspaper for sales, subscribed to the (now defunct) Grocery Game, and was an avid coupon clipper. One of her favorite memories was the time when she got a cart full of groceries for only ten cents. With a totally straight face, her husband pulled a dime out of his pocket and said, "Here, let me pay for the groceries this week." They still laugh when they remember the look on the cashier's face.

Rebecca comes by her frugality honestly. Her parents were born during the Great Depression and knew how to make money stretch. In contrast, her husband was raised in a family comprised of good, hardworking people who didn't always handle money well. Money often went out faster than it came in, and her husband carried those habits into their marriage.

Rebecca developed an "If you can't beat them, join them" attitude, and before their first child was born, they were deeply in debt. Thankfully, while her husband still leans toward spending and Rebecca leans toward saving, after more than 30 years of marriage, except for their mortgage, they are debt free. They have a weekly budget meeting and a monthly meeting to review their big-picture financial goals. Their marriage is evidence that even financial opposites can learn to live together in harmony.

Much of the success with saving money comes down to mindset. How you view money impacts your attitude toward money, your attitudes impact your actions, and your actions ultimately lead to financial success or failure.

On the other hand, Steve *isn't* a naturally frugal person. While he pulled himself out of debt in his early 30s, his financial mindset for many years was to always look for ways to make more money. But his mindset shifted when he met his wife and learned from her experiences about the positive, cumulative effect of looking for small savings in all aspects of life.

Moreover, Steve <u>fully embraced</u> the idea of saving money once he discovered a concept commonly known as *Financial Independence*. (We'll talk more about this concept in a later section.) Now Steve has become a convert to the philosophy of saving money on the unimportant stuff and putting the difference into long-term assets that will provide security for his family.

In the following pages you will discover a wide range of suggestions that both Steve and Rebecca have used in their journey to saving more money. And while we're on the topic, let's review what we actually cover in this book.

Finally, neither Steve nor Rebecca are licensed financial advisors. The financial, and more specifically, investment information in this book is simply intended to provide an overview of some of the most popular options. Please do your own research or consult a licensed financial advisor before making significant financial decisions.

About *Stack Your Savings*

As a reminder, the core principle of the stack your savings concept is to create a series of small wins that will add up to a lot more money in your pocket. So we've broken down this book into four key sections:

First, there is the introduction, which you're currently reading.

Next, we'll discuss the seven pillars of the stack your savings habit. Whenever you're in doubt about what to do with your finances, you can use these concepts as a guideline of what to do next.

Third, we'll talk about *where* to put your money, specifically how to create short- and long-term goals that match what you want from life. You will learn about: the trick to structuring your savings, different investments to consider, and how to create a simplified money plan that works for your personal situation.

Fourth, we'll dive into the bulk of the book, where we'll talk about what we call the "five money levers." These are the important categories of your life where you will get maximum results by focusing on saving money. In other words, we *won't* talk about the small gains that make little difference. Instead, we'll show you how to identify the big picture items and discover major savings.

To give you an idea of what you'll cover, here are the five money levers:

1. **Credit cards and your credit score:** Like it or not, the amount of debt on your credit scores and your overall credit score can have a massive impact on your ability to sock away as

much money as possible. So with this money lever, we'll provide you with a two-prong strategy to reduce your credit card debt and improve your credit score.

2. **Home ownership:** Whether you rent or own a home, the costs associated with this expenditure will often be your highest monthly bill. In this money lever, we include a variety of tactics you can use to reduce this cost.

3. **Insurance:** In addition to home insurance, there are a variety of loans that can quickly add up to a *lot* of money each month. But with a few small tweaks, you can easily reduce many of these monthly expenditures.

4. **Meals:** As a society, the amount we spend on food has spun out of control. Fortunately with a few simple lifestyle changes, you can quickly curb the amount that's spent on meals.

5. **Life Expenses:** This last money lever is a mixed-bag of simple tactics you can use to cut a few financial corners without it negatively impacting the overall quality of your life. In this section we cover everything from saving money on your cell phone bill to building specific habits that will help you save money with every purchase.

Finally, we'll wrap up everything you'll learn with the five money levers and show you how to turn this information into action.

Simply put: There is a *lot* of information in this book, so you might be unsure about how to get started. With this last section, we'll provide a step-by-step framework to help you pinpoint the strategies that will help you the best and then incorporate them into your busy schedule.

You'll find that *Stack Your Savings* doesn't have a lot of fluff. Instead, we get right to the point and provide you with the tools to keep a little more cash each month. So, with that in mind, let's talk about the seven pillars of the stack your savings habit.

HOW TO SAVE MONEY:

A PLAN THAT ACTUALLY WORKS

7 Pillars of the Stack Your Savings Habit

As we just mentioned, there are a *lot* of ideas included in this book. So you might find yourself struggling with what to focus on first. That's why before we dive into the strategies, we think it's important to focus on the seven pillars of the stack your savings habit. Consider these pillars to be the basic guidelines you can turn to whenever you agonize over an important financial decision.

Let's get to it.

Pillar 1: Work on Your Biggest "Pain Points"

If you've read other money-saving books and blogs, you've no doubt seen suggestions for ways to save a penny here and a penny there. While there may be some merit to that approach, we want big wins! Rather than helping you save pennies; our goal is to empower you to save large amounts of money with minimal effort.

Focus on Dollars, NOT Pennies

Proponents of saving pennies often quote Benjamin Franklin, who in his *Poor Richard's Almanac* wrote, "A penny saved is a penny earned." While at first glance it may seem that Franklin advocated penny-pinching, according to The Free Dictionary, [2] the meaning behind this saying is the "money that you save is more valuable than the money that you spend right away." It's all about delayed gratification, and putting money aside for future use.

---

2   https://idioms.thefreedictionary.com/penny+saved+is+a+penny+earned

We, on the other hand, love the British saying, "penny wise and pound foolish" which cautions against obsessing over saving small amounts of money while at the same time being careless with larger amounts of money. You have limited time and energy, so rather than exhausting yourself by working day and night to save a few pennies, we want to help you focus on saving money on the big things.

For instance, some people drive 20 miles to save $0.10 per gallon on gas. They may save $2.00 doing so, but when you consider the time it takes to drive the 40 miles roundtrip, they're essentially "working" for around $3.00 an hour.

Over the course of a year, this money-saving tactic wastes around 40 hours of time, or an entire week's worth of work for a savings of just a little over $100.

Want an easier and more eco-friendly approach? Then it would make more sense to invest in a fuel-efficient car where you'll save money on gas with every mile you drive!

Look for Maximum Results with Minimal Effort ...

If you want to get maximum results with minimal effort, we recommend applying the 80/20 rule,[3] also known as the Pareto Principle. Named after Italian economist, Vilfredo Pareto, the basic idea is that in economics, 80% of results come from 20% of your efforts. While Pareto's focus was on economics, the same truth applies in almost every area of life—including saving money.

With that in mind, while there are countless ways to save money, in our opinion, it's better to focus your efforts on the biggest buckets of your life.

---

3   https://www.developgoodhabits.com/80-20-rule/

For instance, according to the US Bureau of Labor Statistics,[4] in 2016 families comprised of at least one parent and one child under the age of 18 spent the following income percentages on consumer expenditures:

- 14.8% on food
- 38% on housing
- 17% on transportation
- 5.1% on healthcare
- 7.5% on personal insurance and pensions

As you can see, the top three consumer expenses are food, transportation, and housing. Because of that, your biggest financial wins can come by focusing on the **most efficient** ways to save money in those three areas.

While not on the above list, it also makes sense to save money by paying off high-interest debt such as credit card debt, as well as on big ticket items such as vacations.

... But Don't Underestimate the Compounding Effect of Small Savings

While we firmly believe in focusing on the biggest money levers, there are times that it makes sense to save money in small things as well. For instance, the savings from washing and reusing plastic bags and hanging clothes out to dry is small, but if you're environmentally conscious, you have more than one reason to do those things, which can make such endeavors worthwhile.

It also makes sense to focus on small wins once you have a solid

4   https://www.bls.gov/news.release/cesan.nr0.htm

grasp on saving money on the big things. We get into this more in Pillar 6.

Pillar 2: Put a Price Tag on Your Time

The mindset of putting a price tag on your time is directly related to Pillar 1, where we talked about focusing on big levers.

To put a price tag on your time, think of every purchase as "units of your life." For example, if you make $20 per hour, a $100 purchase means you spent five hours of your life to purchase that item. (The time cost is even higher when you consider taxes and credit card interest.)

Here's a practical example. After work, you decide to take your family out to dinner. Let's say that the dinner costs $60. Would it be worth spending an extra three hours at work to pay for that dinner? When you think of it from that perspective, you may decide it's easier to go home and prepare a simple meal. This is especially true if you consider the time it takes to get everyone in the car, drive to a restaurant, wait to be served, and then drive home.

To take putting a price tag on your time a step further, consider the true cost of recurring expenses.

For example, paying $100 more a month on apartment A versus apartment B may not seem like a big deal, but that adds up to $1,200 a year. If you're in the apartment for three years, that's $3,600. At $20 an hour, that would be 180 hours of extra work to pay the higher rent. Only you can decide whether the slightly nicer apartment is worth the extra work.

To calculate the value of your time:

1. Start with how much you're paid each month (before taxes).

2. Divide this by the number of hours you spend working. Don't forget to include your commute time!

3. Write down this hourly wage and put it in a prominent location.

Once you've put a price tag on your time, get into the habit of considering the true cost of the item whenever you're tempted to make an unnecessary purchase.

Pillar 3: Stop Thinking "I Deserve It"

Based on numbers from the US Census Bureau and the Federal Reserve, the average US household has $16,883 of credit card debt[5] and $29,539 in car loans. When you add those two numbers together, the total average debt (not counting a mortgage) of an American family is $46,422. When you add in student loans of $50,626, that number rises to $97,048. When you contrast that with the median income of $59,039, it's clear that the average American family lives beyond their means.

There are many possible causes of spending more than you make, and except for true hardships such as big, unexpected medical bills, you can avoid most of them. Here are a few tactics to help you live within your means.

5 https://www.usatoday.com/story/money/personalfinance/2017/11/18/a-foo lish-take-heres-how-much-debt-the-average-us-household-owes/107651700/

Overcome the "I Deserve It Mindset" and the Comparison Trap

We get it. You work hard. You like nice things. And sometimes you just need a break. But just because your neighbors, coworkers, or family members have or do something doesn't mean you NEED—or deserve—those things.

For example, perhaps most people you know think nothing of picking up dinner on the way home from work. You may reason, "I work just as hard as they do. I'm tired, and I deserve a break." That "I deserve it" mindset may lead you to swing through the drive-through on the way home even though you have to put it on your credit card because you don't have the money in your budget for dinner out.

Those small, unplanned purchases add up, and it's even worse when you make impulsive or image-based decisions that carry a hefty price tag.

Last year Rebecca and her husband replaced the windows in their home. It was a true need, as in the winter, no matter how much they ran their heater, their home was always uncomfortably cold. One of their friends noticed the window installation and came over to chat. After admiring the windows, she stated that she'd love to do the same, but for financial reasons needed to wait a few years. Surprisingly, just a few months later, the friend had new windows installed—ones that were "more high-end" than those Rebecca and her husband purchased. Granted, we never know someone else's motives. Perhaps she actually had the money for them and truly needed new windows. However, it's possible that she succumbed to the comparison trap, also known as "keeping up with the Joneses."

Perhaps you yourself have given in to the comparison trap or bought things because someone else did, or because you wanted to impress others. On two occasions, Rebecca purchased brand-new, high-end phones and computers before important client meetings. The particular clients were very image conscious and on the materialistic side. At least on a subconscious level, she wanted to project a successful image and felt that showing up with the latest and greatest tech gadgets was a way to prove her worth. She now realizes the foolishness of that and has a goal of waiting at least five years to replace those items, unless they break before then.

Avoid the Lure of Instant Gratification

The key to taking massive action and successfully building the money-saving habit is to avoid the lure of instant gratification, which essentially means that you want something, and you want it NOW. In contrast, delayed gratification means to put off something that is mildly pleasant now to gain something more rewarding later.

Saying no to instant gratification in favor of delayed gratification can happen on both small and large scales. For instance, on a small scale, you may choose to stop or reduce multiple fast-food purchases in a month to instead go out to a nice restaurant at the end of the month or to save up for a vacation.

On the other hand, an example of delayed gratification on the largest scale is to reduce unnecessary expenditures for a long period of time in order to retire with dignity 20 or 30 years from now.

Naturally, there are many examples in between those two extremes. For instance, you may see something you want to buy, and instead of buying it right then and there, make a commitment to wait 30 days. At the end of the 30 days, you may decide you still want it, and therefore purchase it, or you may realize you don't really need it after all.

Now that we've covered the basics of instant gratification, let's get into the reasons we succumb to it in the first place and how to overcome this tendency.

Eliminate the "Impulse Buying" Habit

One of the most common forms of instant gratification comes in the form of impulse buys. Impulse buys are often small-ticket items that you had no intention of buying when you went to the store.

According to the Association for Consumer Research,[6] research on impulse buying began in the 1950s and continues to this day. Most of us know of the perils of impulse buying, and yet even the most frugal among us succumbs to it at times.

For example, Rebecca readily admits to occasionally grabbing a magazine or cheap cookbook while in the checkout line at the grocery store. Her husband tends to buy breath mints or candy. Those are inexpensive items, but when unchecked, those little purchases add up and can really blow a budget.

If we know that impulse buying is bad, *why* do we do it? Here are some reasons to consider.

> Shopping Addiction: For some people, just thinking about buying something makes them feel good. Not wanting that

---

6   http://www.acrwebsite.org/search/view-conference-proceedings.aspx?Id=7206

excitement to go away, they purchase the item, even if they don't need it.

Fear of Missing Out (FOMO): If others are buying the new hot product or service, you may be tempted to buy it because you don't want to miss out. For instance, if a new restaurant opens in town, and you see a line going around the block to get in, it's natural to want to get in line just to find out what all the fuss is about. Rather than simply hearing about the latest gadget, you want to experience it yourself. This is especially true when it comes to popular trends such as the latest iPhone.

Loneliness: While this motivation for impulse buys may be uncommon, it's a real problem for some. Stores have people, and for some who have few friends, a store with kind and helpful employees may meet the need to interact with others, but they're a dangerous place for impulse buyers.

Frugality: Yes, even frugal people give in to impulse buys. This happens most often when things are on sale. For instance, if you see a designer outfit that costs $1,000, but it's 75% off, how can you pass up such a great deal? The problem is, you may not need the outfit. Even worse, you may not even really like it, and because of that, it ends up sitting in your closet, unworn. Maybe you'd never spend money on that designer outfit, but you can't resist buying produce or baked goods that are marked down. Those marked down goods are marked down for a reason, and if you're not intentional, they'll go bad before you have a chance to eat them. Marked down grocery items that you end up tossing aren't such a good deal after all.

Since succumbing to impulse buys can blow your budget, keep you from saving for more important things such as a home purchase or retirement, and prevent you from developing good financial habits, it's important to get a handle on them. To avoid impulse buying, follow the tips below.

- **Create a 30-day waiting list for big purchases.** When you see something you'd like to purchase, instead of buying it now, add it to a list (with today's date). If you still want to buy it a month later, as long as you have the money in your budget to do so, go for it! Chances are, once the immediate desire wears off, you may decide not to purchase the item. If that's the case, pat yourself on the back for avoiding the unnecessary purchase.

- **Avoid unnecessary visits to shopping areas.** Many people go to the mall to hang out with friends, or to kill time. Going to the mall without a specific purpose is an almost guaranteed way to buy things you don't really need. If you do need to go to the mall, go with a specific purpose in mind and focus on that purpose.

  - For example, if you need to buy a pair of shoes, head directly to shoe stores or the shoe department of various department stores. Don't walk into stores that don't sell shoes, and don't browse in other departments.

- **Find free or inexpensive ways to reward yourself.** It's good to celebrate accomplishments. However, instead of celebrating by blowing money, look for free ways to celebrate.

  - For instance, when Rebecca completes a big goal, she often rewards herself with a spa day at home. And whenever Steve achieves a major milestone in his business, he treats himself to a movie (instead of going out and blowing his money on a major purchase).

- **Avoid online shopping websites and TV channels.** Shopping channels have a singular purpose—to get you to buy something that perhaps you don't even know you "need." Those channels present merchandise in such a compelling manner that you may feel you can't live without the item— even though you've been living without it just fine!

  ○ The same is true of shopping websites, particularly since they know what you've purchased in the past and suggest other things you may be interested in. There are some exceptions to this. For instance, Rebecca discovered that she spends less on groceries when she orders them online and either has them delivered or goes to the store to pick them up. When she orders online, she isn't tempted by items not on her list.

- **Stick to a shopping list.** Before going out, make a shopping list that consists only of items you need. When shopping, focus on getting the items on the list without stopping to look at other things.

- **Stop using credit cards.** The use of credit cards enables you to buy things now and worry about the consequences later. The problem is that when the bill comes in, you may not have the money to pay them off, and because of that, your budget is blown.

  ○ Frequent credit card use can eventually lead to an inability to pay even basic bills. If you find yourself unable to control the use of credit cards, remove them from your wallet. You may even want to put them into a water-filled container that you keep in your freezer so that you can't use them without first taking the time to thaw. If even that doesn't work, after building up a basic emergency fund of $1,000, cut up the cards.

- **Do research before making a purchase.** Especially when it comes to large expenditures, it makes sense to research before making the purchase. Research slows down the buying process and gives you time to think through the purchase, not to mention find out pros and cons of the product.

- **Consider how every purchase impacts your goals.** Every purchase you make has the potential to move you away from your goals, including goals that have nothing to do with finances. For instance, when you buy something that isn't part of your budget, you spend money that you could put toward something that's more important, such as your retirement account or saving for a vacation. A non-monetary example is that when you make an unhealthy food purchase, it impacts your health and fitness goals.

The impulse buying habit can make or break your ability to save money for your short- and long-term goals. So if you frequently have trouble with controlling your financial urges, then we recommend overcoming this habit before implementing any other idea in this book.

Pillar 4: Create Goals Related to Savings

Saving money for the sake of saving money is not only boring, it can even demotivate you if you don't have an underlying reason to stay on the path. Because of this, it's important to have very specific short- and long-term financial goals.

When you set your goals, be sure to attach numbers to them.

For example, Steve aims to have between $20,000 and $30,000 in savings before purchasing a rental property so he can make a 20% down payment on the property.

Rebecca focuses on dividend growth investing and sets goals related to monthly dividend payments. Since dividend growth investing is a "get rich slow" approach, rather than initially focusing on the amount she needs to retire, she instead sets goals such as getting enough dividends each month to pay for certain bills. She started with a small goal of $125 per month in dividends that will cover the electric bill and is working her way up to bigger figures such as enough in dividends to pay her mortgage.

Goals don't have to be as lofty as saving for retirement or for down payments on rental properties. As explained in our book, *The Budgeting Habit: How to Make a Budget and Stick to It,*[7] the You Need a Budget app[8] has a goal feature that provides a way to save up for financial goals both big and small.

For instance, Rebecca has goals established for saving set amounts by a specific date toward vacation, computer

---

7   https://www.amazon.com/Budgeting-Habit-Budget-Develop-Habits-ebook/dp/B07F8J6DKP

8   https://www.youneedabudget.com

replacement, and for annual subscriptions such as web hosting. Each time she looks at her budget she is reminded of how much she needs to allocate toward the goal to stay on track and have enough money set aside by her self-imposed deadlines. When you set up goals in this way, it's easy to stay on track with your budget because every purchase is in direct competition with your goals.

In addition to setting savings goals, you can set up goals for a certain amount of income through a side-hustle, or for putting aside a set amount each month in your child's college fund.

Regardless of the type of goal, it's vital to have a specific purpose for the goals.

For instance, going back to Steve's goal of saving $20,000–$30,000 for a down payment on a rental property, the purpose of that goal is to put 20% down and therefore not have to pay PMI (Principle Mortgage Insurance).

Rebecca got motivated to set dividend payment goals when she came to grips with the fact that her husband will likely pass away before she does, and if he does, his pension will "pass away" with him. She's decided that dividends are the best way to make up for that lost income. When she thinks about what it would be like living without that income, she's willing to sacrifice financially now as it enables her to face her future with confidence.

Financial goals are so important, in addition to providing information on different levers for saving money, we'll help you create specific goals that will keep you on track when you feel that lure to spend unnecessarily.

Pillar 5: Automate as Much as Possible

It may seem counterintuitive, but often the best habit you can build is to remove certain decisions from your life. Setting up automatic withdrawals from your primary checking account is one of the best ways to meet your financial goals and obligations.

For instance, Steve automates monthly payments like his mortgages (on both his personal and investment properties), all his utilities, deposits into his investment accounts, and other recurring bills. In fact, the only bills that aren't automatically paid are his credit card bills because he likes to review these statements each month.

Here are some other things to automate:

1. Contributions to your retirement account
2. Contributions to your child's 529 education account
3. Weekly or monthly transfers from checking to savings to gradually build or replenish your emergency fund

When it comes to automation, to avoid any nasty surprises, periodically review any bills you've automated and adjust for things such as increased prices. Rebecca came close to having her Internet cut off when they raised the price without her realizing it. Since she paid her Internet bill automatically and didn't realize the price had increased, she underpaid a couple of months in a row. Thankfully, since she reviews her bills on a regular basis, she caught the under-payment before it was too late.

If you automatically transfer money from checking into savings, be sure to leave enough in checking to cover your monthly spending. The Federal Reserve has a savings withdrawal limit of six withdrawals in a single month. Transferring funds from savings to checking counts as a withdrawal, even if the accounts are in the same bank. If you make more than six withdrawals in a month, your bank may charge you a fee. This regulation exists to position banks to have adequate reserves on hand and to encourage people to use savings accounts for saving, rather than regular spending. Budgeting[9] is one of the best ways to ensure you always leave enough money in your checking account. You can also make a point of leaving a $500 buffer in your checking account to cover any unexpected expenses or financial miscalculations.

In addition to the above safeguards, it's important to avoid a "set it and forget it" approach to automation. Start by automating just one or two items initially, and once those are humming along nicely, add a bit more financial automation to your process. It also helps to review all of your automatic payments at least once every quarter and adjust as needed.

Pillar 6: Small Wins Do Matter

While we've chosen to focus on big wins in the book, small wins DO matter. Once you have savings on the big money levers in place, check yourself for thoughts that may creep in such as, "It's only a few bucks, so cutting it out of my life won't make a difference."

To understand how those small expenditures add up, let's do the math.

---

9   https://www.amazon.com/Budgeting-Habit-Budget-Develop-Habits-ebook/dp/B07F8J6DKP

$100 a Month

With just a few small changes, you can easily save an additional $100 per month. Instead of blowing that money, what if you put it into an investment account that earns 8% per year? An article on Investopedia, "Investing $100 a month in stocks for 30 years," shows the math. To quote:

> [if a] 30-year-old investor finds a way to save an additional $100 per month. He contributes the extra $100 to his portfolio and keeps reinvesting his dividends and interest payments. His investment still earns 8% per year. For simplicity's sake, assume compounding takes place once per year in January.

> After a 30-year period, thanks to compound returns and a small monthly contribution, his portfolio will grow to $186,253.14 (as compared to $50,313.28 without the monthly contributions). While $186,253.14 is not enough money to retire on, especially after 30 years of inflation, remember that this is just with $100 a month in contributions and returns below historical averages.

> Suppose the annual return is 9%, which is closer to historical averages for a 30-year period. With a $5,000 principal investment and $100 monthly contributions, the portfolio grows to $229,907.44. If the investor is able to save $200 a month for contributions, the future value of his portfolio is $393,476.48.[10]

We share this example not to push you to put everything into investments. The point we're trying to make is that when you

10   https://www.investopedia.com/articles/investing/100615/investing-100 -month-stocks-30-years.asp

commit to saving money on those small recurring charges, these wins really start to add up!

Pillar 7: Fully Commit to the Stack Your Savings Process

We all know people who are perpetually broke. Rebecca has a friend who has cut out things like cable, and had some other large reductions in her bills, and yet her financial situation is just as dire today as it was three years ago. As shared in our book, *The Budgeting Habit*,[11] Rebecca was once so down due to finances, had it not been for her kids, suicide would have been an option. Perhaps you haven't hit that point of despair, and yet you can't seem to dig out of your financial hole. Maybe you've made some solid financial improvements but still feel you are in a perpetual cycle of two steps forward, one step back.

The bottom line is that there will be setbacks. There will be days when you just don't want to save money or when you have unexpected financial upsets such as car trouble. The only way to see results is to push through those times and save money in spite of your feelings or circumstances. This ongoing, daily struggle is why we emphasize the habit part of saving money.

You need to be all in **and commit to practicing the principles we cover** every single day.

One tool that can help you stay committed is AmericaSaves.org. In addition to getting some great content on how to save money, and reading encouraging testimonials, you can take things a

---

11   https://www.amazon.com/Budgeting-Habit-Budget-Develop-Habits-ebo ok/dp/B07F8J6DKP

step further by making a pledge[12] to "save money, reduce debt, and build wealth over time." You can also sign up for emails and text messages to help you stay on track with your savings goals.

Speaking of goals, in the next chapter we'll dive into setting some big-picture savings goals.

---

12   https://americasaves.org/for-savers/pledge

What Is Your Savings Goal?

As a society we've been programmed to be consumers. Many of us have developed an almost insatiable need to have the latest and greatest gadgets in our lives. This problem is nothing new. No doubt you're familiar with the idiom, "money burns a hole in your pocket" which means to spend money as soon you obtain it. According to Idioms.online, this saying dates back to the 1840s, and around 300 years before that, Thomas More said, "Having a little wanton money, which him thought burned out the bottom of his purse."[13]

While this concept is clearly nothing new, the human tendency to spend money as fast as it comes in is exacerbated by the number of advertisements we see on a daily basis. According to Jay Walker-Smith,[14] the president of the marketing firm Yankelovich, "we've gone from being exposed to about 500 ads a day back in the 1970's to as many as 5,000 a day today."

With the human nature to spend coupled with the constant bombardment of ads, how do you keep money from "burning a hole in your pocket"? The key is to transition from a spender mentality to a saver mentality.

To keep things simple, let's look at each using a simple formula:

Spenders: Income – Expenditures = Savings

Or ...

Savers: Income – Savings = Expenditures

---

13 https://www.idioms.online/money-burns-a-hole-in-your-pocket/

14 https://www.cbsnews.com/news/cutting-through-advertising-clutter/

Spenders get money in, spend it, and if there's anything left, they save it. In contrast, when savers get money in, they first put money into savings and then use whatever is left for their expenditures. This has also been popularly referred to as "paying yourself first."

Our goal in this section is to help you flip the script and become someone who focuses on saving instead of spending.

As an example, Steve is happy to drive his beat-up Honda Civic that he purchased in 2010. It's not a fancy car, but he avoids spending money on a new one because he feels his other financial goals are more important.

One key component to transitioning from a spending to saving mentality is to make your decisions based on the purpose of the item. For instance, rather than a way to impress others, the real purpose of a car is to get you from point A to point B. Therefore, reliability, not flashiness, is the primary requirement for a car.

Pay Yourself First

As mentioned earlier, the formula:

Income – Savings = Expenditures is often referred to as paying yourself first.

According to Investopedia,[15] paying yourself first is:

> A phrase popular in personal finance and retirement-planning literature that means automatically routing a specified savings contribution from each paycheck at the time it is received. Because the savings contributions are

---

15   https://www.investopedia.com/terms/p/payyourselffirst.asp

automatically routed from each paycheck to your savings or investment account, you are paying yourself first. In other words, paying yourself before you begin paying your monthly living expenses and making discretionary purchases.

Where to Pay Yourself First

Having a specific goal in mind can be the difference between spending or not spending money on an impulse buy.

For example, since Rebecca wants to retire with dignity, she set a goal of maxing out her ROTH IRA each year. She pays herself first by automatically sending $125 per week to her retirement account. She chose that figure because since she's 50+, she's allowed to contribute $6,500 per year into her Roth IRA. If you do the math, you'll see that $125 x 52 = $6,500. Alternatively, she could accomplish the same goal by investing $541.66 once a month, or $270.83 twice a month. When she considers her future, it's easy to prioritize retirement savings over discretionary spending.

Here are some examples of short- and long-term goals that you can accomplish by paying yourself first.

Short-Term Goal 1: Build an Emergency Fund

More than 50% of Americans have less than $1,000 in savings, and close to 40% have no savings at all.[16] Without money in savings, even a small emergency such as the hot water heater going out is a crisis. Bigger emergencies such as job loss have an even greater impact.

---

16   https://www.cnbc.com/2017/09/13/how-much-americans-at-have-in-the ir-savings-accounts.html

Since emergencies happen to everyone, building an emergency fund should be your first consideration. We recommend having a bare minimum of $500–$1,000 in savings, with the goal to gradually save up enough to cover three to six months of your expenses.

Short-Term Goal 2: Eliminate Short-Term Debt

Once you have $1,000 in savings, due to the high interest rates, paying off credit card debt is your next priority. Not coincidentally, this is the first money lever we'll tackle in this book.

Student loans and car and home improvement loans are other examples of short-term debt.

If you're not in debt, consider setting some short-term savings goals such as saving for down payments on investment properties, home improvements, or a dream vacation. If you want to break free from your day job or just want to make some extra cash, consider setting aside funds to start a side-hustle.

You can also invest in index funds, but it's important to know that since the stock market goes up and down, you should be prepared to hold on to your investments for a minimum of five years. Stock market volatility is yet another reason to save up three to six months expenses in a regular savings or money market account. A good amount of cold hard cash will reduce your stress and help you to stay the course if your other investments plummet.

Long-Term Goal 1: Retire with Enough in the Bank

Regarding the best time to start saving for retirement, there's no time like the present! If you're in your twenties, it may be hard to imagine and feel motivated to start saving for something that you won't experience for 40 years! But due to the power of compounding, those who put off saving for retirement until they're older have a hard time catching up to those who save even modest amounts on a consistent basis early on.

Here are six types of retirement accounts to consider:

1. **401(k) or 403(b)**, which are offered by your employer. These are the most common and best ways to start, particularly if your employer offers a match. For example, if your employer matches up to 3%, you want to invest at least 3% of each paycheck into your employer-sponsored retirement account. Failing to do so is like throwing away free money! The great thing about 401(k) and 403(b) accounts is that the contributions are automatically deducted from your paycheck, which is the ultimate way of paying yourself first! Another plus is that you can invest up to $18,000 of your pre-tax income (or $24,000 if you're 50 or older).

2. **Solo 401(k)** is a great option for those who are sole proprietors or in a partnership with a spouse. With this account, you can invest as both the employee and employer for total contributions up to $53,000 (or $59,000 if you're 50 or older).

3. **SEP IRA** is another retirement account option for self-employed individuals. (SEP stands for "Self-Employed Pension.") Contributions are limited to a maximum of 25% of your net income or $53,000, whichever is *less*. These accounts are easier to set up than a solo 401(k) and often

offer more investment options than the solo 401(k). Note that if your business has employees, if you contribute to your account, you must also contribute to their accounts as well.

4. **Traditional IRAs** allow contributions of up to $5,500 per year (or $6,500 per year for those age 50 and older). You can contribute to both a 401(k) and a traditional IRA, but there are limitations on tax write-offs.

5. **Roth IRAs** also allow contributions of up to $5,500 per year (or $6,500 per year for those age 50 and older). Note that if you contribute to both a traditional IRA and a Roth IRA, that your total IRA contributions cannot exceed $5,500 (or $6,500 for those 55+). Roth IRA contributions grow tax-free and are a good option for those with an income of less than $116,000 (single) or $183,000 (married filing jointly). Most consider a Roth IRA to be preferable to traditional IRAs so long as you meet the income limitations.

6. **Health Savings Accounts (HSAs)** can be a good option for those with high-deductible health insurance plans. Individuals can contribute up to $3,350 per year, and families can contribute up to $6,500 per year, tax-free. Those 55 and over can contribute an additional $1,000. You may use your HSA to pay for medical expenses such as copays and glasses. Money not used rolls over from year to year. Once you hit age 65, you may use the money for any purpose, but any money used for anything other than medical is taxable.

Long-Term Goal 2: Fund Your Children's Education

There are three primary options for saving toward your children's education.

1. **529 College Savings Plans** are the most popular college savings options. The contribution limits vary by state and range between $100,000 and $350,000 per year, with no income restrictions. Parents are the primary account holder and are in control of the money. The disadvantage is that the funds can only be used for college, and there are stricter investment options than many of the other investment options. Contributions are not tax deductible, but the money in the account grows tax-free.

2. **Coverdell Education Savings Accounts** are more flexible than 529 accounts in that they can be used as early as elementary school, all the way up through college. You may contribute up to $2,000 per year. Contributions are not tax deductible, but the money in the account grows tax-free. In contrast to 529 College Savings plans, once your child reaches the age of 18, they receive control of the account and can use it as they please. If they withdraw it and use it for something other than education, there are penalties.

3. **UGMA Custodial Accounts** are more flexible than 529 and Coverdell accounts in that they can be used for anything including but not limited to education. UGMAs allow parents or other relatives such as grandparents, friends, or even the child to make contributions. Each parent can contribute up to $14,000 each year without paying a gift tax. Since UGMAs are more flexible than the other savings options, they are a great way to give your child a head start on having funds available for a car, starting a business,

world travel, or a down payment on a home. Since the funds can be used on anything, UGMAs are an especially attractive option for children that may opt out of college.

While the flexibility has many advantages, there are also drawbacks. The main one is that from day one, the money belongs to the child. This may disqualify the child from receiving financial aid. In addition to that, parents have no legal control over how the child uses the money once he reaches the age of 18 (or 21, depending on the state), even if the child uses the money in frivolous or even dangerous ways.

Long-Term Goal 3: Pay Down Your Mortgage

Saving for a down payment on a home is one of the most common and most important savings goals for most people. Depending on season of life, interest rate, and level of debt aversion, saving money in other areas of life so you can pay extra on your mortgage can be a valid financial goal.

Long-Term Goal 4: Financial Independence

Financial Independence (FI) has gained popularity in recent years. The basic goal here is to create enough "assets" in your life so that you don't need a job to pay for your lifestyle. FI has many of the same characteristics as a traditional retirement, but most fans of this strategy shoot for this goal *decades* before the traditional retirement age.

People approach this goal in different ways. Some choose to live very simple and frugal lives to accelerate their progress toward this goal. Others with higher incomes may choose to live a "normal" life but sock away more money than their peers.

On the other hand, Steve's FI goal is a mixture of building

businesses, writing books (like this one), buying rental properties, and socking away all extra earnings into long-term investments through low-cost index funds offered by Vanguard.[17]

Okay, we'll admit that the last paragraph barely scratches the surface of financial independence. So if you'd like to learn more about this concept, we recommend checking out the "getting started" page provided by the ChooseFI blog and podcast.[18]

17 https://investor.vanguard.com
18 https://www.choosefi.com/welcome-to-financial-independence/

How to Structure Your Savings

Many people have just one bank account for their entire life. This is problematic in several ways.

First, having all of your money in one account makes it too easy to spend it all. You look at your checking account balance, see there is money in it, and conclude you have money to go out to dinner or make some other unnecessary purchase. Before you know it, your balance is lower than ideal, and when a bill comes in, you may lack the funds to make the payment. On top of this, it leaves you with no plan for emergencies or other unforeseen events.

Also, unless you use a budgeting program such as You Need a Budget,[19] having only one account also makes it nearly impossible to track where you're spending your money. This is the exact opposite of the smart way to save money, as it encourages you to spend first and save later.

The solution is to create a framework where you have multiple accounts, each with a specific function, that match both your short- and long-term goals.

Here's what we recommend:

1. **Checking Account 1:** Deposit all income into this account. From there, have preset amounts that are automatically pulled from the account and put into other accounts that we list below.

2. **Emergency Fund Savings Account:** Regardless of your short-term or long-term goals, the first type of savings you

---

19   https://www.youneedabudget.com/

should focus on is an emergency fund. The initial goal here is to save up at least $500–$1,000. Once you hit that goal, continue to add to this account regularly until it gets up to at least three months' worth of expenses. Emergency funds are meant for emergencies. To avoid dipping into them, give some thought ahead of time into how you define an emergency. You can read more about emergency funds here.[20]

3. **Additional Savings Accounts:** In addition to your emergency fund savings, it's important to save up for short- and long-term goals. Consider this type of savings as a regular expense, as important as bills, loans, and other mandatory expenditures. To simplify things, you might want to consider using payroll deductions to automatically fund these accounts or set up an automatic monthly deduction from your checking account.

   Our advice is to have a separate savings account for each of your short-term and long-term goals. For instance, you may have a savings account for vacation, car repair and replacement, and home improvement. One glance at the account balance lets you know how much you've saved up to spend on those items.

4. **Checking Account 2:** This second checking account is the one you use to pay your bills. This is the account that money flows out of regularly, so be sure to maintain a balance that is sufficient to pay routine bills, groceries, eating out, and other regular expenses. To streamline things, set up automatic bill pay for fixed expenses. It's also important to create a habit where you pay non-fixed bills on a weekly

---

20   https://americasaves.org/for-savers/set-a-goal-what-to-save-for/save-for
-emergencies

basis. As you pay your weekly bills, take a few minutes to review your budget to make sure you're on track with your spending.

The exact number of bank accounts you use and the way you use them is unique to every person or family. To give you some idea of how this works, here's how Rebecca and Steve do it.

Example A: Rebecca's Family

Between Rebecca and her husband, they have the following eight accounts:

1. **Business PayPal Account:** About half of Rebecca's business income is deposited into her PayPal account. As it comes in, she transfers it to her business checking account. Since she generally doesn't use PayPal to pay any bills, she maintains just a $100 balance in this account.

2. **Business Checking Account:** The other half of Rebecca's income is automatically deposited into her business checking account. From here she automates the payment of recurring bills such as life insurance and automated deposits into her retirement accounts. She also automates moving money from checking into savings on a regular basis to save up for things such as a new computer.

3. **Business Savings Account (1):** Since Rebecca uses YNAB (You Need a Budget) to keep track of how much she has saved for various things, she needs just one primary savings account. This primary account houses her business emergency fund as well as savings for things like a new computer. One glance at her YNAB account tells her how

much she has saved for each item since every penny is allocated to a specific budget savings goal.

4. **Business Savings Account (2):** Rebecca's second business savings account is what she refers to as her "profit" account. Each month she deposits 5% of her business income into this account. Each quarter, when she pays her quarterly tax estimates, she does something fun with half of what's in her profit account. Over time the balance of this account grows and acts as a secondary business emergency fund.

5. **Joint Personal Checking Account (1):** This checking account is the first of four joint accounts with her husband. Her husband's paychecks are deposited into this account. Rebecca also transfers a set amount from her business checking account into this joint account each month. This is the primary account they use for paying bills. They use YNAB to break this account into various buckets, so they are sure they always have enough to pay bills.

6. **Joint Personal Checking Account (2):** Rebecca's husband is semi-retired and works just half the year. Because of that, during the months he works, they move half of each of his paychecks into this checking account so that it's "out of sight, out of mind." In the months when he isn't working, they transfer a "paycheck" from this account into their joint personal checking account 1.

7. **Joint Personal Savings Account:** This savings account is their short-term savings account. It includes their emergency fund and other "sinking" funds such as money they are saving toward vacations and HOA special assessments. They use YNAB to keep track of how much is in each savings bucket in this single savings account.

8. **Joint Vanguard Money Market Account:** As extra money comes in, Rebecca and her husband add money to a joint money market account. This acts as a longer-term emergency fund as well as savings for big projects such as home renovations.

In addition to the accounts listed above, Rebecca and her husband each have retirement accounts. Rebecca also has a business credit card that she pays off each month from her business checking account.

Example B: Steve's Family

Steve follows a slightly simpler process with six accounts for his family:

1. **Business PayPal Account:** Like Rebecca, Steve sees a sizeable amount of monthly business income flowing into his PayPal account. And also like Rebecca, he immediately moves this amount into his business checking account.

2. **Business Checking Account (1):** The rest of Steve's business income flows directly into his business account. During the first few days of each month, Steve uses this money to pay all outstanding bills like his business credit cards, full-time virtual assistants, co-authors (like Rebecca) and his brother (who is a co-owner on a couple of online businesses with Steve). Once all outstanding bills are paid, Steve transfers money into his personal checking account.

3. **Business Checking Account (2):** As mentioned before, Steve owns a couple of investment properties. So in order to protect his personal life (and other businesses), he owns all these properties in a separate LLC and bank account.

This means whenever money flows from one of his tenants, Steve holds it in this checking account and uses the leftover income to pay down the mortgage on his properties.

4. **Personal Checking Account:** This checking account is singularly owned by Steve. In this account, he has a series of automatic withdrawals that pay for bills, his son's 503b college education plan, and long-term investments into Vanguard. Almost everything here is automated (besides his credit cards), so Steve does very little thinking about "where" to put money.

5. **Joint Personal Savings Account:** This savings account is one that Steve and his wife share. They use this money for long-term goals like improving their home and saving up for fun vacations.

6. **Emergency Funds in Betterment:** Betterment[21] is a popular robo-advisor platform that makes it super simple to get started with investing. While Steve puts the bulk of his money in Vanguard, he keeps a small emergency in Betterment (with a "Smart Saver" account, which offers a 2% interest rate), for the <u>true</u> emergencies that might come up.

One more thing: You might have noticed that Steve and his wife only share one joint account. This is where the *personal* part of personal finance factors in. Steve and his wife both realized a long time ago that they were control freaks when it comes to finances. While they trust each other to never make dumb purchasing decisions, they also like to maintain a little independence when it comes to money.

---

21   https://www.betterment.com/

And that's the main point behind showing you these two examples—there is no "right" answer when it comes to structuring your various accounts. What works for one person would be overwhelming for another. So feel free to use these examples as a general guideline, not as THE way to structure your finances.

Now, these are just two examples that we use, if you'd like to see *one more* example, check out this article, "Using Multiple Bank Accounts to Control Your Spending,"[22] which has an example of a money map that can help you plan out the structure of your different accounts.

As you can see from these three examples, there are different ways to use multiple bank accounts to structure your savings. Take some time to brainstorm and plan out how this approach will work for your unique situation. If you're new to this, start with just a few accounts, and add more as necessary. Later in this book we cover budgeting, which will help you go even deeper with dividing your money into specific buckets.

How Much Should You Save?

One question you may have is, "How much should I save each month?" Some people say 20% and others 10%. To keep things simple, we recommend you start with a short-term goal of putting away 10% of what you earn. Don't worry if this seems too challenging! Throughout this book, we'll provide a series of strategies to trim your spending.

If you feel that you don't have any money to save, check out various programs available for low-income individuals and families.

22 https://www.moneyunder30.com/multiple-bank-accounts-to-control-spending

For example, one option is Individual Development Accounts[23] (or IDAs). The basic idea behind these accounts is that they match money you save toward specific goals. Typically, you receive at least $1 for every $1 you save, and sometimes much more. They assist you in saving for things such as a down payment on a home, education, or starting a business. Each state has different opportunities, so be sure to do a bit of digging to find out which option is best for you.

Or if you are on Medicare, see if you qualify for a Medicare Savings Program.[24] One of Rebecca's elderly friends qualified and receives $134 per month added to her social security check.

The key thing to figuring out how to structure your savings is to *just start*. Even if you currently don't put any money into savings, start with just 1%, and gradually increase the percent. Every time you have a bit of extra money come in, put at least part of it away. Remember, even $100 per month invested can have an amazing compounding impact!

Okay, now that you understand how to structure your savings, let's dive into the specific places where you can put your money.

---

23   https://prosperitynow.org/everything-you-need-know-about-individual-development-accounts-idas#ques1

24   https://www.medicare.gov/your-medicare-costs/get-help-paying-costs/medicare-savings-programs

Where to Put Your Money

While we've spoken in broad terms about how to structure your savings, we have yet to dive into the specific vehicles that can hold your extra money. To be honest, there are thousands of options—each with their own pros and cons. So it's easy to feel overwhelmed. Since few people can do it all at once, it's important to prioritize and classify what's important right now and what can be postponed for the future when you have more money in the bank.

So we'll keep things brief and *only* talk about a few popular options. And then we'll close out the section with a variety of resources you can use to get more information.

Short-Term Savings

We'll define *short-term savings* as any financial goal you set for less than five years. If you plan to use the funds in five years or less, it's important to use a safe or "mostly safe" option.

Option A: Banks and Credit Unions

A 100% safe option is a standard savings or checking account at your bank or credit union. Banks and savings and loans are insured by the Federal Deposit Insurance Corp, commonly referred to as FDIC. Federal credit unions are not insured by the FDIC; however, they are insured by the National Credit Union Administration, or NCUA. As such, any funds you put into your bank or federal credit union are insured, which means you don't have to worry about losing the money you add to those accounts. They are also completely liquid, which means you can access the funds at any time without penalty.

The downside to these accounts is that they pay minimal interest and because of that don't even keep up with inflation. If you don't mind forgoing the convenience of being able to walk into the bank up the street, consider online banks, which tend to pay a bit higher interest than brick-and-mortar banks.

In spite of the low-interest rates, since there is no risk and since they are liquid, they are an excellent place to stash cash that you may need to access quickly, such as your short-term emergency fund.

Option B: Certificates of Deposit (CDs)

Like savings accounts, Certificates of Deposit (commonly referred to as CDs) are FDIC insured, so they are a safe investment. The difference between CDs and regular checking and savings accounts is that in exchange for a slightly higher interest rate, you agree to let the money sit for a specified period of time.

For instance, if a CD has a one-year term, if you touch the money before the term expires, you pay a penalty. This can be advantageous if you want a bit of extra motivation to hold on to money longer term.

A CD ladder is one popular strategy for those who invest in CDs and yet want to access this money without penalty in case of emergency. The basic concept of CD ladders is that you buy new CDs on a regular basis so that they mature at different times.

For instance, you may buy one CD this month, one next month, and so on. If you purchase CDs that mature in a year and do this consistently, within a year you have a new CD maturing each month. Alternatively, you can purchase CDs with different term limits such as one that matures in five years, the next one matures in four years, and so on and eventually end up with one maturing each year.

Unless you need the disciplinary benefit of not being able to touch money for a period of time, CDs generally only make sense if you purchase them when interest rates are high, so you get a better rate. Otherwise, most find savings accounts with higher interest rates to be a better option for things like a long-term emergency fund.

Long-Term Savings

Investment accounts, including but not limited to retirement accounts, generally work best as a long-term option. We define long-term as five years or longer. These investments tend to have a bigger reward—but also a bigger risk.

For instance, if you invested all you were saving toward a down payment on a home into the stock market in 2007, hoping to buy your home in 2008, you may have seen your investment vaporize, along with your dreams of home ownership. In contrast, if your investments had a drastic drop in value in 2007 but you didn't plan to access them until 2014 or beyond, you had time to recover any losses.

It should be noted that there are some safer options in investment accounts. One example is PIMCO's Enhanced Short Maturity Active ETF[25] (ticker MINT). At the time of this writing, the year-to-date performance is 1.3%, which isn't great, but it also currently has a 2% dividend. The dividend is paid monthly, and if you choose to reinvest the dividends, it's an easy, relatively safe way to grow your nest egg.

---

25   https://www.morningstar.com/etfs/arcx/mint/betaquote.html

Now, since investing is a separate topic that is best covered by licensed financial advisors, we won't dive too deep into this topic. However, below are some apps and brokerage firms we've found helpful, along with a few investing books and YouTube channels that we both like.

Web Resources

- Use this calculator[26] to determine the maximum you can contribute to different retirement plans, including a 401(k), IRAs, and SEP IRAs.

- IRS Guidelines on Gift Taxes[27]

- Vanguard Investment Options[28]

- Acorns[29] rounds up your purchases on the credit and debit cards you link to the app. The difference is automatically transferred to an Acorns account. Since it rounds up purchases you make, it's a great way to invest if you feel you can't afford to invest. Acorns charges $1 per month for accounts under $5,000. Once your account balance hits $5,000, the fee is .25% per year.

- Betterment[30] is another low-fee robo-advisor. Steve uses this for his emergency fund. Like Acorns, Betterment has an annual fee of .25%. This is a great tool if you want to dip your toes into investing *without* having to worry about picking a specific stock or index fund.

---

26   https://sepira.com/calculator.html
27   https://www.irs.gov/businesses/small-businesses-self-employed/frequently
-asked-questions-on-gift-taxes
28   https://investor.vanguard.com/investing/investment-accounts
29   https://www.acorns.com
30   https://www.betterment.com/

- Wealth Front[31] is another robo-advisor that offers financial advice and automated investments in such a way that it reduces risk and minimizes your tax burden. The cost is a flat .25% fee.

- Stash Invest,[32] like Acorns, is a great way to start investing if you want to be able to invest in small increments. You can start with as little as $5. Stash allows the purchase of fractional shares of exchange-traded funds (ETFs) and individual stocks. There are no trading fees. Instead, Stash charges $1 per month for investment accounts or $2 per month for retirement accounts with balances of less than $5,000. Once an account balance hits $5,000—as with Acorns, Betterment, and Wealth Front—Stash charges an annual fee of .25%. Rebecca has both an investment account and a Roth IRA account with Stash.

- M1 Finance[33] is gaining popularity for good reason: there are no fees, regardless of account size. Investment accounts require $100 to start, and retirement accounts require an initial investment of $500. In addition to no fees, another unique feature of M1 Finance is that you create a pie (or multiple pies) that allocates a certain percentage toward each ETF or stock. Each time you invest, the funds are automatically allocated according to your specified percentages. Rebalancing is also automated.

- Robinhood[34] is a favorite of many investors since it has no trading fees and no monthly fee. However, there are a few drawbacks. For example, at the time of this writing, there

31 https://www.wealthfront.com/
32 https://www.stashinvest.com/
33 https://www.m1finance.com/
34 https://robinhood.com/

are no retirement accounts, you can't buy fractional shares, and there's no option to automatically reinvest dividends.

- Vanguard[35] is the king of solid, low-cost ETFs. There are no trading fees for ETFs, and other than low expense ratios associated with the ETFs, no ongoing fees. Steve uses this for his SEP IRA and long-term growth, specifically investing in VTSAX, Vanguard's total stock market index fund. Rebecca has a Roth IRA and joint investment account (with her husband) at Vanguard.

- If the financial independence topic that we talked about previously sounds interesting to you, then we also recommend these blogs and podcasts: Choose FI,[36] Mr. Money Mustache,[37] and Mad Fientist.[38]

Books

- *Dividend Growth Machine*[39] by Nathan Winklepleck is one of the books Rebecca read when first getting started with dividend growth investing. It's a good starting place for understanding the benefits and ins and outs of investing in dividend stocks.

- *Automatic Income*[40] by Matthew Paulson lays out the basics of dividend growth investing.

---

35   https://investor.vanguard.com/home/

36   https://www.choosefi.com/

37   https://www.mrmoneymustache.com

38   https://www.madfientist.com/

39   https://www.amazon.com/Dividend-Growth-Machine-Supercharge-In
vestment-ebook/dp/B01ASEVGYG/

40   https://www.amazon.com/Automatic-Income-Dividend-Investing-Gener
ate-ebook/dp/B01MSHW39X

- *The Bogleheads' Guide to the Three-Fund Portfolio*[41] by Taylor Larimore is a great book for those who want a simple, proven investment plan using low-cost ETFs.

- *Millionaire Teacher: The Nine Rules of Wealth You Should Have Learned in School*[42] by Andrew Hallam

- *The Simple Path to Wealth: Your road map to financial independence and a rich, free life*[43] by JL Collins

Courses and YouTube Channels

- *Build a Passive Income Dividend Portfolio in 12 Easy Steps*[44] is the most helpful and comprehensive educational option Rebecca used to learn the ins and outs of dividend growth investing.

- The Independent Investor[45] YouTube channel teaches how to build a solid investment portfolio without hiring an investment pro.

- Ryan Scribner's[46] channel covers investment basics along with some solid personal finance advice.

- YouTube channel PPC Ian[47] provides solid investing advice for dividend growth investing.

---

41 https://www.amazon.com/Bogleheads-Guide-Three-Fund-Portfolio-Out performs-ebook/dp/B07DH1QYJK

42 https://www.amazon.com/Millionaire-Teacher-Wealth-Should-Learned /dp/1119356296

43 https://www.amazon.com/Simple-Path-Wealth-financial-independence -ebook/dp/B01H97OQY2

44 https://skl.sh/2Bub2UT

45 https://www.youtube.com/channel/UCWKapSw_Przw9W7Hc-zgddg

46 https://www.youtube.com/channel/UC3mjMoJuFnjYRBLon_6njbQ/fea tured

47 https://www.youtube.com/channel/UCXtrYuGksGkkyls50lPWvYQ

Regardless of the type of investment apps or approach you use, it's important to see saving and investing as a marathon, rather than a sprint. Since it's impossible to time the market, those who buy and sell frequently tend to lose money over time compared to those that focus on dollar-cost averaging, which simply means to invest small amounts consistently.

Okay, now that you understand *where* to put your money, let's dive into the five levers that will help you create the stack your savings habit.

MONEY LEVER 1:

CREDIT CARDS AND YOUR CREDIT SCORE

Why This Money Lever?

The biggest money lever you can pull is the dual strategy of improving your credit score while paying off your credit cards. Get these two strategies right and you'll be miles ahead of most people who struggle with their personal finances.

So let's start by talking about why you should focus on both at the same time.

Benefits of Paying Off Credit Card Debt

Typically, credit cards have much higher interest rates than any investment over the long haul. The average credit card interest rate is at an all-time high of 16.7%.[48] In contrast, when adjusted for inflation, the annual rate of return of the S&P 500 is approximately 7%.[49] Additionally, paying off your credit card is a guaranteed way to keep from paying all that interest, as opposed to no guarantees with money you invest in the stock market.

In addition to saving money on interest, when you pay off your credit cards, it frees up massive amounts of money to invest in more important things. For instance, if you currently pay $500 per month on credit cards, consider what else you can do with that money once you pay off the cards.

Here are two examples, one relatively short-term, and the other very long-term.

If you put $500 each month in a savings account that pays

---

48   https://www.usatoday.com/story/money/personalfinance/2018/05/04/avera ge-interest-rate-new-credit-cards-hits-record-high/577238002/
49   https://www.investopedia.com/ask/answers/042415/what-average-annual -return-sp-500.asp

1% interest annually, over the course of five years, you'd save $30,606.03. (Without any interest, you'd have $30,000.) Depending on where you live, that could make a nice down payment on a home or a remodeling project on a home you already own.

Now let's look at the long-term option of investing that $500 per month in a retirement account. At the end of 30 years, at a modest interest rate of 6%, you'd have $474,349.12.

There are much better ways to spend $500 each month than paying credit card bills!

Benefits of Improving Your Credit Score

Now let's talk about your credit score. There are several benefits to improving your credit score. Here are the top nine benefits.

1. Lower interest rates on credit cards and loans
2. Increased odds of qualifying for credit cards and loans
3. Approval for higher loan amounts
4. Increased odds of being approved for apartment or home rentals
5. Lower car insurance rates
6. No security deposit needed when applying for a cell phone contract
7. No security deposit when signing up for utilities
8. Increased odds of qualifying for a business loan to start or expand a business
9. Increased odds of getting a job (many prospective employers check applicants' credit scores)
10. Greater likelihood of qualifying for a home loan at a better interest rate

Have these benefits convinced you of the importance to focus on your credit and credit cards first?

If so, then we'll start by covering the top methods for paying off credit cards, and then we'll dive into how to improve your credit score.

How to Save on Your Credit Cards

Step 1: Know Where You Are

The first step in paying off your credit cards is knowing where you stand. To do so, we recommend a two-pronged approach.

First, pull out all of your credit card statements (or look them up online). Jot down the balance you owe on each card, along with the interest rate.

Second, head over to the credit.com credit card payoff calculator[50] to find out how long it will take you to pay off the card(s), based on different payment amounts. Here are a few examples of how this works.

If you have a credit card with a $1,000 balance at 11% interest and pay the minimum payment of $20 per month, it will take you five years and eight months to pay off the card, and the total amount you pay will be $1,344. Now let's say you decide to hit it harder and pay $100 per month. You'll make 11 payments and thus pay it off in a bit less than a year, and the total amount you pay will be $1,054. Let's ramp up the payments even more and pay $250 per month. In that case, it will take you five months to pay it off, with a total paid amount of $1,024.

If you have only $1,000 of credit card debt, you're fortunate. The average household credit card debt[51] (of those who have credit card debt) is $9,333! With that in mind, let's use the same credit card calculator to compare different payment amounts.

---

50   https://www.credit.com/tools/credit-card-payoff-calculator/
51   https://www.valuepenguin.com/average-credit-card-debt

For the sake of this example, we'll divide the $9,333 equally between the three cards, for a balance of $3,111 on each card.

Card #1 has an interest rate of 11%, card #2 has an interest rate of 13%, and card #3 has an interest rate of 15%.

Using the calculator, we can see that the minimum monthly payment on card #1 is $60, $65 on card #2, and $70 on card #3, for a total minimum payment amount of $195 per month. Paying the minimum payment on each card, by the time you pay them off you will have paid $13,227 over the course of five years and eight months.

Since we used $500 as the figure for what you could accomplish financially if you didn't have credit card debt, for the sake of example, we'll assume that you have $500 per month available to pay on your credit cards.

Later in this chapter we'll get into two popular credit card payoff strategies. For now, let's divide the $500 between the three different cards to see how quickly you can pay them off paying $167 per month on each of the three cards. At that rate, you'll pay off the $9,333 of debt in one year and nine months, for a total of $10,481 in payments.

As you can see with the above scenario, upping the amount you pay each month on your cards saves you $2,746.

Step 2: Come Up with Extra Money

Regardless of which of the credit-card payoff methods you choose, if you have a lot of debt to pay off, it's easy to become discouraged and give up. Even if you're a plodder and have the discipline to stick with something long-term, it's advantageous to pay off debt sooner rather than later. One of the best ways to do that is to come up with extra money. The remainder of this book is chock full of simple strategies you can use to trim money from your budget.

Use the money you trim from your budget and apply extra amount toward paying off your credit cards. For example, once you're saving $100 or $200 dollars per month, take ALL this money and us it to pay off your credit cards faster.

Remember that some of the interest rates can be over 15%, so it would be impossible to find a better place to put your money than getting rid of debt that's crippling your financial future.

Step 3: Use **Smart** Balance Transfers

Transferring what you owe on a high-interest rate credit card to another credit card with a lower (perhaps even 0%) interest rate can help you pay less interest and ultimately enable you to pay off your credit cards faster. While this is appealing and can certainly make sense financially, it's important to carefully read the fine print before making the transfer.

Here are a few things to watch out for:

First, there is almost always a transfer fee. The transfer fee is typically a percentage of the balance transfer. For instance, if the balance transfer fee is 3%, you'd pay $300 on a $10,000 balance transfer.

Second, the introductory rate is for a limited time, most commonly 12 months. After that time, the rate goes up, often to a higher rate than the card you transferred the balance from.

Third, if you are late on any of the payments, you may immediately go from 0% interest to a high rate.

Fourth, balance transfers may improve your credit score, but they also have the potential to have a negative impact on your credit score. For more information, check out the Investopedia article, "How do balance transfers affect my credit score?"[52]

The bottom line is that balance transfers only make sense if you've already established some financial discipline and can ideally pay off the amount you transfer before the introductory rate expires.

Step 4: Choose the Right Method to Pay Off Your Credit Cards

Once you've determined that it's time to focus on paying off your credit cards, it's important to do so strategically.

Here are three methods to consider.

1. Debt Avalanche Method

With the debt avalanche method, you focus on first paying off the credit card with the highest interest rate, regardless of the balance on the card. If you choose this approach, list all of your credit cards according to the interest rate, with the card with the highest interest rate at the top of the list and the card with the lowest interest rate at the bottom.

The advantage to the debt avalanche method is that you typically pay off your total debt faster and pay less total interest. The disadvantage of this method is that if the balance on the highest

---

52   https://www.investopedia.com/ask/answers/111714/how-do-balance-trans fers-affect-my-credit-score.asp

interest rate card is high, it can take seemingly forever to make progress, and out of discouragement you may give up. Because of that, this method is best for those who are more analytical and patient and don't mind it taking awhile to see a big win.

2. Debt Snowball Method

The debt snowball method was popularized by Dave Ramsey.[53] In contrast to the debt avalanche method, you list your debts from smallest to largest and attack the smallest one first, regardless of the interest rate. You then focus on the next smallest one until you pay it off and continue with that approach until you pay everything off.

The advantage to this method is that you experience quick wins, particularly if you have some credit cards that you can pay off within a few months. Those wins can put the wind in your sails and motivate you to keep going, since you see success early on.

The disadvantage with the debt snowball method is that it can take longer to pay off all your credit cards and you'll pay more interest than you would with the debt avalanche method.

3. Debt Tsunami Method

This lesser-known *third* option, which may or may not include credit card debt, focuses on paying off emotional debts first. For example, debts owed to friends and family members tend to be emotional due to your personal relationship with the lender. These loans often have a low or even 0% interest rate, so mathematically it doesn't make sense to pay them off first. However, they also often have a high cost in terms of strained

---

53   https://www.daveramsey.com/blog/get-out-of-debt-with-the-debt-snowba ll-plan

relationships with the people who matter most to you. Because of the high emotional toll, it can be advantageous to pay these loans off as fast as possible.

Consistency Mixed with Flexibility

While we generally advise consistency in any plan you follow, you may decide to do a combination of methods. For instance, you may have an emotional debt that you simply want to get off your back, three credit cards with relatively low interest and lower balances, and one credit card with a high balance and higher interest rate.

Depending on how you're wired, you may find it helpful from a psychological perspective to knock out the emotional debt, then the lowest balance card before switching over to the debt avalanche method. Knocking out a couple of the less mathematically logical debts first may give you the momentum you need to attack the higher interest rate card with a big balance.

Make a Plan and Stick with It

While some flexibility is okay and can even be advantageous, rather than jumping from one method to the next, it's important to make a plan and stick with it. When making your plan, consider your personal temperament, along with the emotional toll various debts have on you. List out the debts in order of importance to you, and then stick with paying things off in that order.

If you feel at all unsure about the proper method for you, we recommend the debt avalanche method since it's the most mathematically sound option.

Note: Regardless of which technique you choose, be sure to

make minimum payments on all of your debts other than the one currently at the top of your priority list.

Step 5: (Optional) Consider Peer-to-Peer Lending

Peer-to-peer (P2P) lending is a way to cut out the financial institution to get a short-term loan. You've probably heard the term "crowdfunding." If not, think of sites such as Kickstarter and GoFundMe, where large numbers of people contribute small amounts of money to help an individual or business meet a funding goal. Peer-to-peer lending employs a similar concept; large numbers of people loan small amounts of money to individuals.

With peer-to-peer lending, you apply for a loan. Next, a P2P business evaluates your financials and then gives you an interest rate, which is often far lower than your credit card rate. People can then invest in your loan. While we generally don't recommend that you go deeper into debt, if you have credit card debt with a high interest rate, you can use a P2P loan to pay off your high-interest credit cards.

There are a few pros and cons to this system.

Pros of P2P Lending

Peer-to-peer loans typically have lower interest rates. Some can go as low 5–6%, which is far superior to credit card rates.

Similar to most of your bills, P2P loans also have fixed payments. All you have to do is stick to the amount every month, and you'll eliminate your credit card debt at a much lower rate. Fixed payments not only make it easy from a budgeting perspective, but you can also automate the payments.

Cons of P2P Lending

Speaking of automating payments, it's a good idea to do that in part due to significant P2P lending late fees. For example, at the time of this writing, Lending Club[54] (one of the two P2P networks we recommend) charges a late fee of 5% of your unpaid balance, or $15, whichever is greater. So if you have a $2,000 balance, and you make your payment late, there's a $100 fine. Ouch!

In addition to late fees, there are also origination fees. The origination fee is the fee that the P2P network charges to activate your loan. This fee is typically anywhere from 2–5% of the loan amount. Obviously, if you're taking out a significant loan for thousands of dollars, this adds up to a pretty hefty amount. Because of this, we recommend calculating the numbers of your existing credit card debt versus taking out a P2P loan.

Additionally, if you have poor credit, you either won't qualify for a P2P loan, or if you do qualify, you will pay a high interest rate. It could even be higher than your credit card interest rate!

Top Two P2P Networks

While new P2P networks pop up on occasion, we recommend either Prosper[55] or Lending Club[56] because they have stood the test of time.

Below are some of the similarities and differences to help you determine which option is right for you.

Both companies require you to fill out an online loan application asking your age, income, employment status and so on. They

---

54   https://www.lendingclub.com/
55   https://www.prosper.com/
56   https://www.lendingclub.com/

then run a credit score check. As we explain later in this chapter, your credit score impacts the interest rate you'll pay on the loan. The interest rate range is virtually the same for each company.

The loans from Prosper range from $2,000 to $40,000, and the loans from Lending Club range from $1,000 to $40,000. Since your loans can be as low as $1,000, if you're unsure about whether to use this option, a small loan may be the perfect option for testing out this debt payoff strategy.

Also, just because they allow loans of up to $35,000–$40,000 doesn't mean you'll qualify for that big of a loan. Your loan approval amount depends on various factors such as your credit score, income level, and your other debts.

Lending Club has an origination fee of between 1% and 6%, and Prosper's origination fee is between 1% and 5%. Both companies take the origination fee right off the top, from your total loan amount. For example, if you borrow $10,000 with a 5% origination fee ($500), the amount deposited into your bank account is $9,500. So keep that in mind if you need a set amount to pay off credit card debt.

Overall, in the same way that you want to take your time before doing a credit card balance transfer, be sure to do your homework before taking out a P2P loan. Since there are more details regarding fees and other terms, and since companies change their terms from time to time, be sure to read the details on the official Prosper and Lending Club websites.

Tools to Help You Eliminate Your Credit Card Debt

Digging your way out of credit card debt takes grit and determination, but many of the tools available nowadays make it a lot easier. Here are our top picks.

Unbury Me[57] has a calculator to help you plan out the best way to attack your credit card debt, using the popular debt snowball and debt avalanche methods we covered earlier in this chapter.

Mint.com Financial Goals[58] is a popular free financial app that will help you get a handle on every aspect of your finances, including paying off debt. It integrates with your bank accounts and will walk you through setting up and achieving financial goals such as getting out of debt.

Undebt[59] is a tool that uses the debt snowball method. It has a calculator and provides a simple-to-follow payment plan once you input your financial information.

You Need a Budget (YNAB)[60] is the tool Rebecca uses on a daily basis to manage her finances. It's what we recommended in our book, *The Budgeting Habit.*[61] We recommend YNAB for the following reasons:

- There's a free 34-day trial, no credit card required. This gives you ample time to test the tool and see if it works for you.
- It's easily customizable.

57   https://unbury.me/

58   https://blog.mint.com/goals/how-to-use-mints-goals-06302010/

59   https://undebt.it/

60   https://www.youneedabudget.com/

61   https://www.amazon.com/Budgeting-Habit-Budget-Develop-Habits-ebo ok/dp/B07F8J6DKP

- It's based on money you actually have rather than estimated income.

- Rather than recording things after they happen, you plan where your money will go before spending it.

- It includes a goal feature to remind you to budget for non-monthly expenditures such as quarterly car insurance payments, computer replacement, or saving up for your dream vacation. You can use YNAB to plan and track your progress on your S.M.A.R.T. goals.

- While some programs automate everything, YNAB makes you account for every dollar that comes in and goes out. Complete automation may seem ideal, but some hands-on work keeps you from checking out.

- You can have more than one budget in your account. For example, Rebecca has a budget for her business and a separate budget for her personal finances.

Trim[62] goes through your credit card charges and finds ways to minimize your recurring subscriptions. It even looks for ways to reduce other bills such as car insurance. Trim will also tell you how much you spent various places in the last month.

For instance, if you tend to binge shop on Amazon, when requested it will tally up your Amazon purchases. This feature can help you see where you blow the most money so you can plug those financial holes. As you reduce or eliminate unnecessary expenditures, you'll have more money and will be able to pay off debt faster.

---

62   http://www.asktrim.com/

How to Save Money by Improving Your Credit Score

Your credit score matters more than you may think! A great credit score will help you with your:

- Home mortgage rates
- Car financing
- Peer-to-peer lending rates
- Real estate investment rates
- Insurance rates
- Loan qualification
- Approval for renting a home or apartment
- Job applications

Simply put, the better your credit score, the more money you'll save in the long-term.

Credit Reports versus Your Credit Score

Before we get into how to improve your credit score, let's first define the difference between a credit report and a credit score. A credit report summarizes your history of debt and bill payments, but it doesn't always include your credit score. Your credit score is a number that is calculated from the information in your credit report. The higher the score, the better.

Now let's dive into how to improve your credit score.

Step 1: Get a Free Credit Report

Under the Fair Credit Reporting Act, you're entitled to get a free credit report once a year. Here are the three major credit reporting agencies:

- Experian[63]
- TransUnion[64]
- Equifax[65]

The problem is that while these credit reports are "free," they often automatically enroll you in an ongoing billing situation such as a "credit monitoring" service. Even worse, once you enroll, you have to call the company and argue until they agree to remove you from the service. Simply put, be very careful when it comes to trying to get a credit report and credit score.

While we're big fans of free stuff, there are times it's worth paying a bit to avoid the hassle. With this in mind, we recommend AnnualCreditReport.com.[66] It's the only website authorized to pull your credit report from all three agencies listed above. While the credit report is free, your credit score is not included. At the time of this writing, the cost is less than $10 to access your credit score. Our advice is to pay a little money and get the damn credit score without worrying about being roped into an ongoing service you don't need or want.

---

63   https://www.experian.com
64   https://www.transunion.com/
65   https://www.equifax.com/personal/
66   https://www.annualcreditreport.com/

Step 2: Know Where You Stand

In your report, find the credit score number from each of the three agencies, which often vary by 10 to 15 points. We recommend either using the average of the numbers or the lowest number as your baseline.

Credit Score Ranges

Credit scores range between 300 and 850.

- 300–579 (very poor)
- 580–669 (fair)
- 670–739 (good)
- 740–799 (very good)
- 800–850 (exceptional)

Our recommendation is to strive for at least a 750, which puts you into the very good range.

Step 3: Make Sure Everything is Accurate

When you get your credit reports, go through each of them to find inaccuracies.

- Is all your personal information (address, social security number, birth date, etc.) correct?
- Are there any missed payments that you know were paid on time?
- Are there any open accounts that aren't yours? (Sometimes this is a sign that you might be victim of identity theft.)

If you spot anything that's inaccurate, you have to talk to each of the credit reporting agencies to fix this issue.

Step 4: Look for Big Wins

There are five factors that comprise your credit score, each weighted differently.

1. Your bill payment history: 35%.

2. Credit utilization: 30%

3. The age of your credit history (how long ago you opened your first credit account): 15%

4. The types of credit on your credit report: 10%

5. Number of credit checks: 10%

Since bill payment history and your credit utilization comprise almost two-thirds of your credit score, you can get a lot of "big wins" by focusing on these areas. Therefore, we suggest a two-pronged approach to improving your credit score, which we go into in steps five and six.

Step 5: Decrease Your Credit Utilization Ratio

Credit utilization simply means the amount of debt you have compared to the credit limit. Your goal is to get this number down to 30% or less.

For instance, if your credit limit on a card is $2,500, aim to have a balance of no more than $750 on that card. Needless to say, maxing out your credit cards has a huge negative impact on your credit score, even if you pay your credit card bill on time.

You can decrease your credit utilization ratio in the following two ways.

First, use the strategies we covered in this chapter to pay more than the minimum on your cards.

Secondly, ask for or accept an increase in your credit card limit. This ultimately means you have less debt (as a percentage) than what you previously had. Every six to twelve months request an increase on your limit.

An important note on this second strategy is to hold off on increasing your credit card limits until you've become more disciplined in your credit card usage. If you've stopped using the cards and are simply focused on paying them off, then by all means, go for increased limits. If you're still struggling with getting a handle on credit card usage, focus on paying down the cards as quickly as possible.

Step 6: Pay Credit Cards on Time

Regardless of any failures in the past, make a commitment to create a great track record of paying your credit cards on time. You can use credit reminders through your online bill account, use one of the apps we mentioned earlier in this chapter, or set up automatic payments.

Rebecca typically pays her credit card in full a few times a month. In spite of that, she has a small automatic payment set up, "just in case." In spite of it being unlikely she'd forget to make a payment, if something unforeseen happens that may distract her from paying the bill, she wants to make sure the payment is made every month.

No matter what, make absolutely sure that you pay *all* your bills on time, every time. While we've focused on credit card payments, do the same for other bills as well. If by chance you have some unavoidable big bills such as medical expenses that you can't pay in full by the deadline, to avoid late payments, do your best to make arrangements to pay the bill in installments.

The more disciplined you are with paying your bills on time, the more your credit score will improve. In fact, if you have a low credit score as a starting point, you have the potential to increase it by up to 100 points by simply paying your bills on time.

Last Thoughts on Your Credit

Improving your credit score can be a big win, but it's also fairly technical. Don't allow that to overwhelm you. You'll see results if you do nothing but pay your bills on time and pay as much extra as you possibly can on your credit cards. If you'd like to dig deeper on the topic, we recommend *Repair Your Credit Like the Pros*[67] by Carolyn Warren.

---

67 https://www.amazon.com/Repair-Your-Credit-Like-Pros-ebook/dp/B00P T0F5QU/

MONEY LEVER 2:

HOME OWNERSHIP

Why This Money Lever?

By now you've probably realized that in this book, we're focusing on the big wins in life.

If you want to save <u>real money</u>, one of the best strategies you can implement is to closely examine every area of your life and look for ways to cut corners on your *biggest* expenditures. And usually the largest "line item" on most people's monthly bills is home ownership (or "rentership" for many people).

Home ownership for many people is more than a third of their monthly income. So being smart about this expenditure will free up money that can be spent elsewhere.

In this section, we'll provide a list of simple strategies you can use to maximize the money you're putting into your home. But first, let's talk about one concept that requires a bit of out-of-the-box thinking.

Think "Geo Arbitrage"

The concept of *geo arbitrage* was made popular by Tim Ferriss in his book, *The 4-Hour Workweek*.[68] The basic idea behind geo arbitrage is that you can live anywhere in the world, and if you choose a place with a low cost of living, your money will go further.

In his book, Ferriss mostly talked about living in inexpensive countries such as Thailand, the Philippines, Costa Rica, or Vietnam and running some form of online business. With a low cost of living, and with an online business, you can fund a lifestyle that others could only dream of. While this is a great concept, it's not an option for most people because they don't want to live outside their country.

But want to know the good news?

Geo arbitrage doesn't mean you have **to live in a third-world country.**

You can even use geo arbitrage to live in less expensive places within your own country. For instance, if you live in San Francisco, London, Oslo, Reykjavik, New York City, or another place with high cost of living, it might make sense to look for opportunities to live somewhere else.

Perhaps you live in a city with a high cost of living but need to stay in the general area due to work or other responsibilities. An intelligent move to a different nearby town can make a difference.

---

68   https://www.amazon.com/4-Hour-Workweek-Expanded-Updated-Cutting-Edge-ebook/dp/B002WE46UW

For instance, Steve and his wife live in Bergen County, New Jersey. Put simply, New Jersey is a *very* expensive place to live, and Bergen County is one of the most expensive counties in New Jersey. To put it in perspective, out of the 30 towns with the highest property taxes, 14 of them are in Bergen County.[69]

Since Steve's wife has tenure and likes to live close to her job, they are limited in options for where they can live. That said, Steve's wife understood the value of living in a town that has low property taxes, so when they moved three years ago, she made sure they moved to a town with one of the lowest property taxes in the area. This decision led to a $5,000 yearly reduction in property taxes. Over a period of ten years, that adds up to $50,000 in savings!

Rebecca and her husband actually considered moving to Thailand. She went to Chiang Mai on a business trip and fell in love with the city. When they found out how inexpensive it is to live there, they were tempted to make the move. Once the impracticality of various aspects of such a move (such as being so far away from family) set in, they scrapped the idea.

However, recently they've been considering a move from their current home in Denver to Colorado Springs, a mere 60 miles away. Housing in Denver is substantially higher than in Colorado Springs.

As an example, the current median home price in her city is $463,255 compared with $272,100 in Colorado Springs. She loves her current home and neighborhood, and she has family nearby. However, her husband plans to retire next year, and they

---

69 https://www.nj.com/politics/index.ssf/2017/02/njs_2016_top-taxed_towns .html

want to be mortgage-free at the time of his retirement, which won't be possible in their current home. They also have a son and daughter-in-law in Colorado Springs, and since housing is so much cheaper there, they'd be able to pay cash for their home. In addition to that, there are multiple military bases in Colorado Springs, and since her husband is retired Army, they qualify for free healthcare and other military benefits in the Springs.

As you can see, every situation is different, so it's a good idea to consider the pros and cons of geo arbitrage. If you decide to focus on geo arbitrage, you can potentially save serious money in the following areas:

- State taxes
- Local taxes (i.e., property taxes)
- Education—specifically college
- Child care
- Commuting costs (tolls, mass transit, parking)
- Food
- Entertainment

Best Places[70] is a good starting point for comparing the cost of living from one city to the next. However, it doesn't include certain costs listed above, such as property taxes. Since property taxes can be hugely different from one state to the next, or as Steve mentioned, even from one town to the next, before making the decision to move, dig deeper to find out the true cost of living.

Also, be sure to consider non-financial costs such as proximity

---

70   https://www.bestplaces.net/cost-of-living/

to family, weather, and crime[71] before making your decision. We also recommend taking at least one "vision trip" to any city you're considering before packing your bags.

We'll be the first to say that geo arbitrage isn't for everyone. Perhaps you love your you're your community, or the proximity to your family. However, especially if you have a big financial goal such as living mortgage-free like Rebecca does, it's worth considering a move to a different town, state, or even country if such a move makes those financial goals possible.

71 https://www.areavibes.com/

2 Options to Reduce Housing Costs

If your housing costs are more than you'd like to spend each month, you have two options here: 1. Stay in your home and look for ways to save money each month. 2. Choose to downsize and reduce your housing costs by renting. Let's go over each of these options.

Option 1: Stay in Your Home

It's no surprise that a mortgage takes a big bite out of your paycheck, but it's important not to allow it to take too big of a chunk. The general rule of thumb is that you shouldn't sign up for anything more than 25–35% of your total household income—even if the bank qualifies you for more.

Buying a home that is below your means frees up more money for other things such as maxing out your retirement account and makes it easier to pay extra toward the principle. This enables you to pay off your home sooner rather than later.

There are a couple of ways to pay off your mortgage faster.

First, you can simply pay a bit extra each month. Start with whatever you can afford, such as paying an extra 10%.

A second option is to make one extra payment on your home per year.

Finally, some people choose to pay half of their mortgage payment every two weeks. Since there are slightly more than four weeks each month, this works out to be 13 months' worth of payments each year instead of 12. This is a great option, especially for those who are paid every other week. It can even make budgeting easier since it divides this big expense into two smaller pieces.

Let's look at how the math works out for each of these options. In each example, we'll start off with a $400,000 home at 4% interest on a 30-year loan. At this level of financing, you'd have a monthly payment of $1,909.66 without paying anything extra.

Strategy 1: Pay Extra Monthly

In this example, let's say you pay $190 per month (or 10%) extra each month. With this scenario, you'd save $51,202.38 in interest and pay off the home four years and eight months faster. To accelerate things, you could pay more than the $190 per month extra any time you have extra funds available.

Strategy 2: One Extra Payment Each Year

With this strategy, you'd pay one extra payment of $1,909.66 each year and save $42,665.01 in interest and pay off your home three years and 11 months faster.

Strategy 3: Biweekly Mortgage Payments

In this scenario, you'll split the $1,909.66 payment in two and pay $954.83 every two weeks. You'll save $45,106.63 in interest and pay off your home four years and two months faster.

From a simple math perspective, the biweekly payment option makes the most sense for a lot of people, particularly those who are paid biweekly. However, not all lenders allow this option, so be sure to check the terms. If you know ahead of time (before you sign for a loan) that you want to implement this plan, make it part of your loan shopping plan.

You can use these calculators to crunch your own numbers:

- https://www.daveramsey.com/mortgage-payoff-calculator
- https://www.mortgagecalculator.org/calcs/biweekly.php

Eliminate (or Avoid) PMI

If you pay less than 20% as a down payment, many lenders require you to get Private Mortgage Insurance, commonly referred to as PMI. This usually runs between 0.5% to 1% of the entire loan amount and can add hundreds of dollars to your payments.

Our advice is to wait until you have 20% of the price of the house saved up before buying. If you're unable to do so and find yourself paying PMI, then the best solution is to aggressively attack the principle on your mortgage by using one of the strategies listed above. Once you get your mortgage balance over that 20% threshold, call your mortgage company to have PMI eliminated.

You can also eliminate PMI in two additional ways. First, you can refinance your home. (More on that in a minute.) You can also have your home appraised and hopefully get a valuation that's higher than when you took out the loan.

Refinance Your Loan

If you purchased your home when mortgage rates were higher than the current rate, refinancing your home can lead to massive savings down the road. This is also a good option if you had poor credit when you purchased your home and have since improved your credit score. Your improved credit score may qualify you for a lower interest rate loan.

You can also use this tool[72] to decide if it's worthwhile to refinance your mortgage.

Downsize Your Home

Downsizing your home is similar in concept to geo arbitrage. You can move into a smaller home that doesn't require a high mortgage, property taxes, or general upkeep. You don't have to live in one of those tiny homes that you see on television, but moving to a smaller home in a different part of town or whole new city can dramatically cut your costs.

While you can use this strategy to reduce your cost while staying in your current city, if you want to turbocharge your savings, consider combining downsizing with geo arbitrage.

For instance, not only are Rebecca and her husband planning on moving to a lower-cost city after her husband's retirement, they also plan to downsize since their current home is larger than they need.

Rent out Part of Your Home

If, like Rebecca, you have more room than you need in your current home but for various reasons aren't ready to move, consider renting out part of your home. Rebecca made the decision to rent out a portion of her home to her daughter and son-in-law.

Her home is a tri-level home, which makes sharing easier, since living spaces are more spread out. She and her husband live in a basement apartment, and her daughter and son-in-law have the entire top floor (three bedrooms and a bathroom) to

---

72   https://www.bankrate.com/calculators/mortgages/refinance-calculator.aspx

themselves. They all share the main level of the home, which includes kitchen, half bath, dining, and living room.

This arrangement provides rental income to Rebecca and a lower cost of living to her "kids." While this arrangement isn't for everyone, it's something to consider if you have more room than you need, are comfortable sharing some of your space, and want help making the mortgage payment.

Use Gabi to Decrease Home Insurance Rates

If you feel like you're spending too much on your home insurance, you can use a service like Gabi[73] that shops around for the best rates on a home and auto policy. All you have to do is link your current home insurance plan and then Gabi uses a computer algorithm to find up to 20 quotes from different companies. And then you'll get a side-by-side comparison to see if you're actually getting the best rate.

Bundle Both Your Home and Auto Insurance Rates

Most major insurance companies offer around a 10–20% discount if you bundle home and auto insurance together. Steve uses USAA[74] to cover both areas of his life (and also his rental properties), which gives him a substantial savings on all his policies.

Overall, it's worth talking to your existing company to see if they offer some sort of bundling option. You might be surprised at how a 30-minute phone call can lead to significant long-term savings.

---

73   https://www.gabi.com/
74   https://www.usaa.com/

Raise the Deductible on Your Home Insurance Policy

A deductible is the amount you pay when you submit an insurance claim. Most deductibles range from $500–$1,000. If you raise it more than that, you'll see a serious decrease in your monthly payment. The main value to the insurance companies with an increased deductible is they know you won't file a claim for minor repairs or small fixes to your home. Obviously, you need to be 100% certain that you have the money to pay your deductible. This is one of the many reasons it's important to build up your emergency fund, like we talked about in a previous section. Avoid raising your deductible until you have enough in your emergency fund to pay the higher deductible.

Build Your DIY Skills

If you do decide to become a homeowner, expect to be responsible for repairing numerous items around your home. If you're not careful, these items can really start to add up. Learning a skill can be fun and a quick way to spend less money. The internet is full of great tutorials and resources. All you have to do is run an internet search for the specific item you'd like to fix, and you'll find a variety of videos and step-by-step tutorials.

For example, Steve once accidentally poured gasoline into the oil tank of his lawnmower. He thought he destroyed the lawnmower and was worried that he'd have to go out and buy a new one. After just a few minutes of watching YouTube videos and applying a bit of elbow grease, he fixed the mistake and now the lawnmower works perfectly!

You can also do the same for home improvement projects.

For example, Rebecca's husband saved them a lot of money by

installing new flooring and tile in their home rather than hiring someone to do the work. He simply watched YouTube videos and then followed the instructions step by step. Not only do you save money, you gain a sense of pride in knowing you can do these tasks yourself.

Option 2: Avoid Home Ownership

We've been programmed to believe that home ownership is an investment since you pay money toward equity. But if you want to avoid a huge money pit, one of the simplest decisions you can make is to rent instead of owning a home.

On the plus side of home ownership, homes typically appreciate in value, and in case of financial emergency, you can borrow against the equity of your home. Home ownership also forces you to save money, since part of your payment goes toward the principle. That said, there are many, *many* "hidden costs" that come up when you own a home—like making minor repairs, fixing or buying new appliances when they break, and taking on lawn maintenance, which costs you either time or money.

On top of the cost of maintenance, in some areas, or during certain economic times, housing values can stagnate, or in some cases, even go down. A home dropping in value for a period of time isn't catastrophic if you plan to stay in your home for a long time, but it can be devastating for those who need to move and are "underwater" (owing more than the current value of the home).

Another consideration with renting versus owning is how mobile you desire to be. If you plan to stay in the same area through thick and thin, and don't have any desire to move even for things like a dream job, then owning a home may be a good option for you. But many people find home ownership to be like a noose around their necks that makes it more difficult to move quickly.

Renting does carry its own risks such as rent going up, sometimes drastically, each time your lease expires. Many people also say that you throw money away when you pay rent. However, that's not necessarily true *if* as a renter you invest the money you would have spent on things like home repairs. If you do that, you'll likely come out ahead financially if you rent rather than own. The problem is that rather than investing any extra money they have as a result of renting, many renters opt to blow it all on consumer goods. If that describes you, and if you plan to stay put for a long period of time, you may benefit from the forced savings that comes through home ownership.

Sure, there are many positive aspects of owning a home. Both Steve and Rebecca own a home, but they do it for personal reasons, not because they believe it's the best use for their money. The key is to be mindful of your big-picture goals, and to make the decision to purchase a home based on how doing so fits with your goals rather than doing it because it's the "right" thing to do.

Well, that covers the simple strategies to save money on home ownership. Now let's talk about one of the more annoying line items on your monthly bill—insurance.

MONEY LEVER 3:

INSURANCE

Why This Money Lever?

Your monthly bills can often look like a bottomless pit. It seems like all you're doing is paying for "stuff" that doesn't positively impact your life in a noticeable way. And even if you eliminate credit card debt and reduce the cost of home ownership, there are many, *many* additional companies with their hands out, asking for your money each month. Specifically, we're talking about the various insurance policies that have become the not-so-fun part of the modern experience.

So if you'd like to continue to look for ways to save *real* money, one of the best things to do is closely examine these major expenditures and trim the fat. Since these expenses occur every month, quarter, or year, taking time to save money on these expenses can add up to some serious savings.

How to Save on Auto Insurance

While there are different factors influencing the steep rates of car insurance premiums, there are numerous strategies you can use to lower your car insurance rates.

1. Get quotes from different firms. Prices of insurance can vary. Get quotes from at least three companies. Your local insurance department may also have a comparative price list for major insurance firms.

When choosing an insurance firm, go to the one that's financially stable. Check the financial standing of the company you're choosing; this information is available in rating company reports and consumer magazines.

2. Tap your connections. Some companies offer discounts on your car insurance if you belong to a professional group (e.g., a teacher's organization) or you're in the military. Insurers like Geico, for example, offer a 15% discount[75] on insurance premiums for servicemen and servicewomen.

3. Compare insurance premiums BEFORE you buy a car. Premiums are partly based on the price of the car, its repair and maintenance costs, its likelihood of being stolen, and its record for safety. Considering these, insurance companies offer discounts for vehicle features that reduce the risk of theft or injury. The Insurance Institute for Highway Safety has a database of safe car models[76] to help you decide what type of vehicle to buy.

4. Increase your deductible. Your car insurance policy will only kick in after you've shelled out a specific amount of money, called

---

75   https://www.geico.com/information/military/
76   https://www.iihs.org/

a deductible. Raising the amount (say, from $500 to $1,000) reduces your premiums by 30% or more. Keep in mind, though, that you must have that amount set aside and available just in case you need to pay when making a claim.

5. Be a safe driver. Drivers without any traffic violations for at least three years of driving (some companies will consider five years) usually have a reduced rate in their car insurance premiums. So, drive defensively and do your best to avoid vehicular accidents while you're at the wheel.

Remember this: Drivers with poor driving records will always be considered high-risk. Accordingly, they will be charged with a higher premium by insurance companies.

6. Reduce coverage on older cars. In addition to the above ideas, if you have a car that is ten or more years old, consider dropping collision and/or comprehensive coverage. Collision insurance helps you replace your car if it gets damaged during an accident. Comprehensive insurance pays for non-collision-related incidents like theft, vandalism, flooding, hail, or fire.

If you have a car that's ten years old (or more) or has a current value of less than $3,000, collision and comprehensive coverage are not going to be of any use. If you drop these, you can save up to nearly $500 annually on collision, as well as almost $200 from comprehensive.

The logic here is that if you have an older car, it may not make financial sense to keep paying for things such as collision insurance. As a general rule of thumb, if your car is worth less than 10X the premium, the insurance isn't worth it. You can look up your car's value on a free website such as Kelley Blue Book.[77]

---

77   http://www.kbb.com

It's important to note that most states require SOME insurance. This article[78] explains the types of car insurance typically required and also gives a list of minimum requirements for each state.

7. Pay your premium in full. Although most people think it's a good idea to pay insurance bills every month, add-on fees for this convenience are usually part of the monthly rate. Instead, request a biannual or annual pay arrangement.

Worried about the lump amount for your car insurance? Try setting up a pay system. Divide the total amount by the 12 months in a year. Set aside that amount every month to make sure you can pay the insurance in full. You can either open up a savings account exclusively for this or use the cash envelope system.[79]

8. Own your vehicle. If you are leasing your vehicle, chances are that you are not in control of how the company who owns the car chooses the insurance. It's more likely the actual car owners will get the maximum coverage for their vehicle, considering that they are letting another person drive it.

So if you want to be in control of what type of insurance coverage you need for your vehicle, buy the car outright.

Car insurance rates will not be going down anytime soon. Driving safely, doing a little research, and making sound decisions that have long-term effects on your choice of transportation can help lower the costs of your premiums.

---

78   https://www.thebalance.com/understanding-minimum-car-insurance-requirements-2645473

79   https://www.developgoodhabits.com/cash-envelope-system/

9. Ask for low-mileage discounts. Do you often work from home? Is your job only five minutes away? Do you carpool with coworkers or use public transportation or ride-sharing services such as Uber or Lyft?

The bottom line is that if you don't put many miles on your car, you can call your insurance company and ask for a low-mileage discount.

10. Ask for additional discounts. While different insurance companies vary, most offer a multitude of discounts you can use to dramatically decrease your car insurance rates. According to DMV.org,[80] there are three kinds of driving discounts:

1. Driver discounts, which include a great driving record, membership in an auto club (like AAA), good school grades, and driver training in an accredited course.

2. Vehicle discounts for cars with specific safety equipment such as anti-lock breaks and airbags, use of alternative fuel, and hybrid vehicles.

3. Policy discounts, which includes insuring multiple cars and paying in full.

There are many types of discounts you can get directly from your auto insurance company. So you should review the above DMV link to get a full listing of all that's available to you. You may also call your insurance company to see what discounts they offer.

---

80   https://www.dmv.org/insurance/3-types-of-car-insurance-discounts.php

How to Save on Health Insurance

We'll be the first to admit that health insurance is a very controversial topic, especially in the United States, where there are very mixed opinions on what's called the Affordable Care Act (ACA), also known as Obamacare. We're not here to debate the merits of ACA. Instead, we'll point out a few strategies you might be able to use to cut costs.

Now, the problem is everybody has their own unique health situation, so some of these strategies won't work in your personal situation, but you might want to give them a shot.

1. Use Policy Genius to shop for health and life insurance. One of the simplest ways to shop for quality health insurance quotes is to use a website like Policy Genius.[81] This is a comparison website that provides quotes from different insurance vendors with side-by-side charts that give you real-world information.

Policy Genius also offers insurance comparisons for other types of insurance such as life, disability, renters, pet, and auto.

When Steve used this site, it only took him a few minutes to find a great life insurance policy that he uses now to protect his family.

2. Open a Health Savings Account. According to Healthcare.gov, Health Savings Accounts (HSAs), are:

> A type of savings account that lets you set aside money on a pre-tax basis to pay for qualified medical expenses. By using untaxed dollars in a Health Savings Account (HSA) to pay for deductibles, copayments, coinsurance, and some

---

81   https://www.healthcare.gov/glossary/health-savings-account-hsa/

other expenses, you can lower your overall health care costs.

This option is only available to those with high-deductible health plans, which are currently defined as deductibles of at least $1,350 for singles or $2,700 for families. In 2018, the contribution limits for singles are $3,540 and $6,900 for families. The great news is, any funds not used one year roll over to the next year, and any interest you earn from the HSA is tax-free.

3. Consider increasing your deductible. Since HSAs are only available for those with high deductibles, and since you generally save money on insurance premiums that have higher deductibles, consider checking with your insurance company to see if you can increase your deductible. Bear in mind, however, that high-deductible plans are best for those in good health. If you, or other family members frequently need to go to the doctor, it may be cheaper for you in the long run to pay a higher deductible.

4. Know what your health insurance policy covers. To avoid nasty surprises, it's important to find out ahead of time what is and is not covered by your insurance policy. If your insurance company has a web portal, be sure to register for an account. Once you log in, poke around a bit and you'll likely find a record of all of your claims. You should also be able to see how much was covered for various office visits, tests and procedures, your copay amount, deductible, and more.

Rebecca discovered that her health insurance portal lists approvals for various preventative care services, such as blood tests and cancer screenings. Along with what is covered, there are eligibility dates for the various tests. When Rebecca found that some of her eligibility dates are later than her doctor feels are necessary, she reached out to her insurance company to find out how to handle that. They let her know how to get approval. Without this knowledge, she could have ended up with a nasty surprise when an unexpected medical bill came in the mail.

5. Beware of balance billing. Balance billing is when a medical provider bills you for the remaining balance of a bill not covered by your insurance. For instance, if a bill was $1,000, and your insurance covered $500, the expectation that you'll personally pay the remaining $500 is known as balance billing.

The important thing to know is that just because you get a bill for the balance doesn't mean you need to pay it. Certain states have laws that prohibit balance billing. However, there are a lot of variables that govern whether or not you need to pay the balance.

For instance, you may be obligated to pay the balance if you go to a doctor that is not part of your network. Since staying in network matters, be sure to choose a primary care physician that is part of your medical insurance network. When referred to another provider for additional medical care, before going to your appointment, double-check to make sure the physician is in your network.

Balance billing is another great reason to set up an online account with your insurance provider. The claims section of your account likely lists each claim, what the insurance company paid, and the amount you are obligated to pay yourself. Rebecca recently found that she paid more than she was obligated to pay for one of her cancer screenings. She contacted the medical provider that improperly billed her and got the amount she overpaid credited to her credit card.

For more information on how to fight balance billing, "Issue brief: Balance billing,"[82] a resource provided by the American Medical Association Advocacy Resource Center.

6. Check medical invoices for mistakes. In addition to the balance billing issue, it's possible there are other mistakes on your bill. For instance, Rebecca's mom noticed that one of her doctors added extra things such as X-rays to her bill. In this particular case, her mom wasn't out the money personally, but the insurance company paid for services not rendered. In the long run, these types of discrepancies impact the overall cost of health care and are worth correcting.

7. Provide test results and records to your doctor. Ask for copies of your medical records, including test results. When you go to a new physician, bring those records along. This may save you from having a recent test repeated.

After Rebecca had a physical for a life insurance policy, she provided the results to her primary care provider, so they became part of her permanent record. When she recently went for a physical, her doctor referred to those records and saw he could skip certain tests.

8. Be on the lookout for local health fairs. Many cities have health fairs that provide free or low-cost tests and services such as flu shots. This is a great way to get services for minimal cost, particularly for uninsured individuals.

9. Consider video or phone consultations. There's nothing that completely replaces in-person doctor visits and tests, but phone and video consultations often cost less than regular doctor visits.

---

82   https://www.ama-assn.org/sites/ama-assn.org/files/corp/media-browser/balance-billing-issue-brief-final.pdf

For instance, Amwell[83] currently charges $69 per visit, which costs less if covered by your health insurance. This is a great option for those who have no insurance, since it's less costly than a typical office visit.

This is also a great option for those who find it challenging to get to a doctor, like if you live in a rural area, have limited transportation, are elderly, or have young children at home.

10. Check out nonprofits that offer healthcare for low-income or uninsured individuals. If you simply don't have health insurance, free or low-cost clinics are your best option. Rebecca's daughter took advantage of one such clinic in Denver in the timeframe when she was too old to be covered by her parents' health insurance but didn't yet have any insurance coverage of her own. She went to a clinic that based payments on a sliding scale. It was a clean, comfortable clinic, and she received excellent care for very little cost.

To find free and low-cost healthcare options in your area, visit FreeClinics.com.[84]

11. Live a healthy lifestyle. While living a healthy lifestyle is no guarantee against illness, you can often reduce, or in some cases even eliminate, your need for medications and other procedures if you eat healthy and exercise.

For example, according to the WebMD article, "What a 5% Weight Loss Can Do for Your Health,"[85] a modest 5% weight loss provides the following benefits:

---

83   https://amwell.com

84   https://www.freeclinics.com/

85   https://www.webmd.com/diet/ss/slideshow-five-percent-weight-loss

- Reduces joint pressure and inflammation, which in turn decreases the odds of developing arthritis
- Decreases likelihood of getting cancer
- Prevents type 2 diabetes—if you already have diabetes, losing weight may enable you to take less medication
- Improves cholesterol levels, which lowers the chance of heart disease
- Reduces triglycerides, which decreases the likelihood of heart attacks and strokes
- Lowers blood pressure
- Improves sleep apnea
- Reverses insulin resistance
- Improves sleep, which helps many other aspects of physical, mental, and emotional health
- Improves moods
- Reduces inflammation
- Improves sex life

In a recent physical, Rebecca found she had a few areas that need improvement. Her doctor recommended that she lose 20 pounds by going on the Mediterranean Diet. Her simple dietary changes will keep her from going on medication anytime soon.

Obviously, healthy eating and exercise don't guarantee good health, but particularly since you can kill several health-related "birds" with one stone, it makes good sense to make this a primary component of your healthcare cost-savings plan.

Well, those are just a few simple ways to save money on the two types of insurance that often eat up your monthly expenses.

Now let's move on to the fourth money lever. This one is often the most insidious expense that people struggle to reduce each month.

MONEY LEVER 4:

MEALS

Why This Money Lever?

According to USDA's Center for Nutrition Policy and Promotion, the average family of four in the United States spends $713.20 for a budgeted food plan.[86] The "liberal plan" that includes a lot of discretionary spending can be as high as $1,000–$1,200 per month.

That $700–$1,200 is a heck of a lot of money to spend just on food. Even reducing this amount by a few hundred dollars each month can amount to *thousands* of dollars you can put toward your short- and long-term goals.

If you'd like to trim the fat on your food expenditure, then one of the simplest strategies you can implement is to plan out your meals for the week—and stick to it. So let's talk about that first.

---

86   https://www.cnpp.usda.gov/sites/default/files/CostofFoodNov2017.pdf

How to Create a Meal Plan—
That You'll Actually Follow!

Meal planning is one of the best ways to reduce food costs because it increases *intentionality* about food purchases. Simply put: Planning your meals ahead of time will reduce the likelihood that you'll make poor food decisions whenever you're tired and/or hungry.

For instance, we've all had those times when we've ordered a pizza or gone out to dinner because we didn't have the ingredients on hand to make a decent meal. With meal planning, you'll make decisions ahead of time (when you're not as tired) that will help you make a smart choice when it's time to eat.

While meal planning requires work upfront, in the long run it saves time since it reduces extra trips to the grocery store, restaurants, and takeout spots. With that in mind, let's dive into an easy meal planning process.

1. Put it on your calendar. The popular saying, "What gets scheduled gets done," is true in many aspects of life, including meal planning. If you realize you need to meal plan right before heading out the door to go to the grocery store, it probably won't happen, so set a time to do it. Ideally, you'll do this the same day every week.

2. Check your calendar. Before creating a meal plan, look at your family's calendar to see if any of the events on it impact your meal plans. For instance, if your kids are in sports, you may want to plan crockpot meals or simple meals you can put on the table in less than 30 minutes on game days. If you're having company, you may want to plan a nicer meal and prepare twice as much food as you normally do.

3. Schedule shopping and prep time. A meal plan does no good if you don't have time to shop. Unless you have a schedule that constantly changes, it helps to make this part of your weekly routine. Many people who work outside the home find it helpful to meal plan on Saturday and shop and prep on Sunday. Others who work part-time or are stay-at-home parents may find it easier to shop while the kids are in school.

4. Decide what you'll serve each day. This is where the rubber really meets the road. You've already decided when you'll meal plan and when you'll shop and prep the food. Now it's time to figure out what you'll serve for each meal.

To up your savings, before planning, browse your local grocery store flyer to see if there are any bargains you want to plan around. For instance, if ground beef is on sale, you may plan to make spaghetti and meatballs, meatloaf, and tacos to take advantage of the sale price.

Many people find it helpful to eat the same basic thing every day for breakfast and lunches during the week, with perhaps something that takes more time on the weekend. For instance, Rebecca makes green smoothies every morning for breakfast, Sunday through Friday, and her husband cooks them omelettes every Saturday. They typically eat leftovers or sandwiches for lunch.

She also likes to have a theme for various nights of the week.

For example, Monday is Mexican, Tuesday Italian, Wednesdays focus on a stew or chili or a main-dish salad (depending on season) and so on.

If you go with themes, try to come up with four to five favorite dishes for each theme that you really like and then just rotate them. For instance, for Mexican night, one week cook tacos, the next week enchiladas, the next week nachos, and so on.

You may also want to plan one day as a leftover day. When her kids were all still home, Rebecca's family had leftovers every Sunday. She pulled all the leftovers out of the fridge and set them up on the kitchen counter, buffett-style. Not only did that give her a super easy meal day, it also ensured that all food was eaten or tossed when it was less than a week old.

5. Make a list. Now that you know what you'll cook and when, it's time to make your shopping list. If you cook the same thing for breakfast or lunch each day, using a recurring list saves time.

For instance, since Rebecca makes green smoothies for breakfast every day, she knows that every week she needs spinach or kale, bananas, and so on. Even though she does this each week, referring to a master "smoothie ingredient list" ensures she doesn't forget anything.

Once you have your regular purchases written down, go through each item on your menu and jot down what you need. Rebecca likes to put a tally mark to indicate the quantity of each item. For instance, let's say that on Monday you need a bell pepper, but you also need one on Wednesday and Thursday; as you go through each recipe, simply add tally marks to indicate quantity.

Don't forget to plan for snacks and treats! You may also want to buy extra sale items to replenish your pantry and freezer at minimal cost.

Before heading out the door, check your pantry, fridge, and

freezer to see if you already have some needed ingredients on hand. Cross those items off your list.

6. Stick to your list! Since you've planned thoroughly and made a list, you'll seldom find a good reason to buy anything not on your list. If you tend to throw junk food or other impulse items into your cart, try eating something before you shop. A growling stomach makes everything look more appetizing.

If you do see something that you forgot to add to your list, ask yourself if you really need it before tossing it into your cart.

7. Do at least basic meal prep. While meal planning and grocery shopping go a long way toward helping you eat more meals at home, since life is so busy, you may occasionally lack the time, motivation, or energy to cook. Even the most basic meal prep done in advance makes cooking meals faster and easier.

In terms of meal prep, Rebecca likes to cut up all of the fresh vegetables she just purchased before putting them in the fridge. Since switching to whole grains that take more time to cook, she now cooks enough brown rice for the week just once a week. She also bags up the ingredients for her morning smoothies and puts them in the freezer.

If you plan to serve two meals during the week that both call for cooked ground beef, cook all the ground beef ahead of time, together with any extras that your family enjoys such as onions and garlic. Toss the ingredients for a crockpot meal into a zippered bag and refrigerate. On the day you plan to eat that meal, first thing in the morning, dump the ingredients into the crockpot. These simple actions enable you to get food on the table in less time, and they also make cleanup a breeze.

Meal Planning Apps

You can certainly use old-fashioned cookbooks and pen and paper to plan your meals, but apps save a lot of time. Sometimes they even make your shopping list for you. Here are some of our favorites (be sure to double-check the prices because they might have changed after this book was published).

- Cozi Recipe Box and Dinner Planner[87] (Free): Available online and as an app, Cozi provides a way to add recipes on the web to your profile. You can then create a shopping list from the recipes and add the recipes to your calendar.

- Mealime[88] (Free): Available for both Android and iOs, Mealime allows you to choose various menu types such as vegetarian, low-carb, or paleo, to name a few. Have allergies or food sensitivities or hate certain foods, like olives? No problem. Simply list those restrictions to eliminate recipe suggestions that don't fit your criteria. Create shopping lists from your selected recipes.

- Yummly[89] (Free): Claims to have one of the most extensive recipe collections. In addition to main dishes, it offers other types of recipes, such as desserts. Like Mealime, you can easily avoid recipes with allergens or ingredients you don't like. One great feature is it integrates with Instacart, so if desired, you can skip the actual grocery shopping.

- allrecipes Dinner Spinner[90] (Free): Has many of the same features as the others, and as an added bonus shows which ingredients are on sale at your local stores. Rebecca

---

87 http://developgoodhabits.com/cozi-family-planner
88 https://www.mealime.com/
89 https://www.yummly.com/
90 http://dish.allrecipes.com/mobile-apps/

especially enjoys the reviews and recipe modification suggestions posted by other allrecipes users.

- Pepper Plate[91] (Free): Allows you to log in and share recipes through email, Facebook, and Twitter and has many of the same features as the previously mentioned apps. One cool extra feature is the ability to put a recipe in "cook now" mode, which includes smartphone timers that remind you to, for example, take something out of the oven so nothing burns up while you're busy with another aspect of the recipe.

- eMeals[92] (14-day free trial, then a monthly or annual fee thereafter): offers multiple menu styles ranging from vegan to paleo to Mediterranean Diet and everything in between. You can switch between meal plan types as often as you want, but you can only select recipes from one plan per week. Each meal plan includes a main dish and side dish. Create grocery lists, order groceries for delivery, or pick up from many different stores. Put the app in cook mode when you're ready to cook, for easy step-by-step instructions on your smartphone or tablet.

- Meal Planner Pro[93] (Free): has a unique focus on various health issues. For instance, if you have high cholesterol, the app serves up heart-healthy recipes. You can set up a profile for each family member, which helps if different family members have different nutritional needs. Each recipe has a "Pro Score" ranging between 1 and 100, based on the nutritional value of the recipe. If you want personalized nutritional advice for you and your family members, be sure to check out this app.

---

91 https://www.pepperplate.com/
92 http://emeals.com/
93 https://mealplannerpro.com/

- Plan to Eat[94] (free 30-day trial, then $4.99 per month or $39 per year): also has a focus on healthy meals. It has a few additional features missing from some of the other apps such as a drag and drop menu planner, planning for leftovers, and the ability to add staples to your shopping list.

- Big Oven[95] (Free, with a pro membership option that runs $1.99 per month, or $19.99 per year): has many of the same features as the other apps. The thing that set this one apart is a focus on leftovers. Want to know what to do with that leftover pot roast, mashed potatoes, and green beans? Input those to find recipes that use those ingredients.

- Supercook[96] (Free): focuses on using ingredients you have on hand. Type in those ingredients to get suggestions. This is great if you want to skip shopping for the week and instead use up what you have in your pantry, fridge, and freezer.

- Budget Bytes[97] (Free, offers in-app purchases): tagline sums it up well, "Delicious Recipes Designed for Small Budgets." This app categorizes recipes by type, such as beans and grains, pasta, slow cooker, etc. One fun feature is that each recipe includes an approximate cost for the recipe as a whole, along with cost per serving. Many recipes also offer ingredient substitution ideas such as swapping out brown rice or another grain for quinoa. These suggestions help you pick a cheaper option if desired, and allow you to use up ingredients you already have on hand.

---

94   https://www.plantoeat.com/
95   https://www.bigoven.com/
96   http://www.supercook.com
97   https://www.budgetbytes.com/

Buy a Deep Freezer

When it comes to saving money on food, deep freezers are like a secret weapon. First, they enable you to stock up on expensive items when they're on sale. Using a freezer to save money works especially well when combined with an aggressive couponing strategy. You can also double up on recipes with ingredients that freeze well, pop them into the freezer, and create your own home-cooked convenience food at a reasonable price.

In addition to that, if you purchased items that will go bad before you can use them, pop them into the freezer to preserve them for later use. Since not all food freezes well, check out this article, "83 Foods to Freeze or Foods Not to Freeze,"[98] for foods that do or don't freeze well.

Obviously, you need space for a deep freezer, but they don't have to be huge. Rebecca has a small freezer in her basement, where she stores meat, homemade convenience foods, and frozen fruit she buys in bulk at Costco. In terms of electricity cost, her small freezer adds less than $25 per year to her electric bill. Most deep freezers cost between $150 and $500, so you don't need to break the bank to buy one.

---

98 https://www.laurengreutman.com/83-foods-to-freeze-or-foods-not-to-fr
eeze/

Use Strategic Couponing to Save on Groceries

In the introduction, Rebecca shared about her grocery shopping exploits that landed her a spot on the local news. Walking out of the store with a cart full of groceries for only ten cents would not have been possible without coupons.

The bad news is, part of Rebecca's success with couponing was due to her Grocery Game subscription, a service that has since gone out of business. The good news is, there are other free coupon sites out there, so you don't have to do all the research on your own. Here are some of our favorites.

- The Krazy Coupon Lady[99] offers a database of more than 4,000 free grocery coupons. The site has a search function that enables you to search for specific brands. Let's say you like Yoplait yogurt and you notice it's on sale at your local grocery store this week. Do a search for Yoplait to find coupons for that brand. It also provides a list of sale items organized by stores with an impressive selection of stores ranging from online retailers like Amazon to grocery stores like Kroger to niche stores such as Yankee Candle.

- Coupons.com is the place to go for coupon codes, cash back offers, and loyalty coupons. It also has a selection of free printable grocery coupons.

- Coupon Mom[100] is the closest substitute for the Grocery Game that Rebecca has found. As a free service, it misses some of the great deals she snagged through the Grocery Game, but it has many of the same features. For instance, it lists deals not just by the store, but by your specific state.

---

99 https://thekrazycouponlady.com
100 https://www.couponmom.com/

Just because an item is on sale in California doesn't mean the same item is on sale in Colorado or New Jersey. It also matches up coupons from the Sunday paper and printable coupons with sale items.

- Honey[101] takes the hassle out of looking for coupon codes that save you money. Some people enjoy the "hunt." They like scouring the Internet, newspaper, and the coupon sites listed above for deals. Others, not so much. If you want good deals without the hassle of searching for coupon codes, this free Chrome app is for you.

- If you want to put your coupon savings on steroids, consider the coupon clipping service, The Coupon Clippers.[102] If you don't want to subscribe to the Sunday paper but want the coupons, buy complete coupon inserts. If you have certain items you buy regularly and want to stock up on them, order coupons for those items. For instance, if you buy a lot of General Mills cereal, do a search for General Mills to find coupons. At the current time, you can get a $1 off coupon for 12 cents. If you don't care about specific brands, search by item type, such as dairy or produce. For best results, buy multiples of the same coupon, and purchase the item in bulk when it's on sale.

---

101   https://www.joinhoney.com/
102   https://www.thecouponclippers.com/

Work Toward Zero Food Waste

Saving money at the checkout stand should be part of every money-savvy shopper's strategy, but it shouldn't stop there. According to a CNBC article, "America's $165 billion food-waste problem,"[103] the average American family throws away as much as $2,200 worth of food each year. Therefore, working toward zero food waste is one of the best ways to save money on groceries.

Here are some tips for wasting less food.

1. Meal plan for fewer meals. If you find that you end up throwing away a lot of food, it could be that you need to plan and shop for fewer meals.

For instance, if you meal plan for seven days per week and end up eating out, some of the food you purchased may go bad.

You may need to experiment a bit to find your sweet spot. Try planning for six days per week, and if you're still throwing food out, reduce that to five. To avoid having the opposite problem of running out of food before the end of the week, keep a well-stocked pantry and freezer with adequate ingredients for makeshift meals.

2. Eat food that spoils quickly first. When you meal plan, be sure to serve meals with ingredients that spoil quickly early in the week.

For instance, fresh basil often goes bad in just a few days, but carrots, cabbage, and sweet potatoes last about a month. Pay attention to expiration dates on dairy products and make a point of using them before they go bad.

---

103   https://www.cnbc.com/2015/04/22/americas-165-billion-food-waste-problem.html

3. Serve smaller portions. It's one thing to eat leftovers that never left the serving bowl, and another to eat food off of someone else's plate—even if they didn't touch it. Because of that, to avoid food waste, serve up smaller portions. If people clean their plate and are still hungry, they can always serve themselves seconds. This tip has the added benefit of reducing overeating.

4. Make a plan for leftovers. Eating leftovers is one of the best ways to avoid food waste and save money on food. Rather than pushing leftovers to the back of the fridge, keep them front and center where you'll see them. Better yet, pack them in travel-friendly containers for grab-and-go lunches. Steve's wife frequently packs her lunch from the leftovers of the meals they prepare as a family.

If you don't like eating the exact same thing more than once, think of creative ways to repurpose the leftovers. For instance, serve chili with cornbread one night, and another night serve leftover chili over spaghetti. Rebecca's family likes an Indian dish made with boneless chicken breasts. The first night she serves it in traditional meal style, with a starch and vegetable. Later in the week she uses the leftover chicken in wraps, and it's a totally different meal with very little work or expense—and zero waste.

Keep a jar or freezer bag in the freezer for leftover vegetables. If you have a small amount of leftover vegetables, instead of tossing them, add them to the container. When the container is full, make vegetable soup.

5. Freeze or dehydrate food before it goes bad. Before freezing or dehydrating, wash produce and cut off any bad spots. Rather than freezing or drying whole fruit and vegetables, slice or dice them to an appropriate size for later use. While this takes a bit of time, you'll appreciate the convenience when it's time to use them. Unless you're going to use frozen foods all at once, freeze individual pieces in a single layer on a cookie sheet before putting into a freezer container. This keeps them from sticking together in one big clump and makes it easier to use just what you need at any given time.

6. Store foods properly. Some foods require refrigeration, and others are better left out on the counter. Check out the article "15 clever ways to make different types of food last longer"[104] for a list of helpful tips.

---

104   https://www.housebeautiful.com/uk/lifestyle/food-drink/a19417308/how
-to-make-food-last-longer/

Identify Your "Latte Factor"

In his book *The Automatic Millionaire*,[105] David Bach talks about a concept that he calls "The Latte Factor." His point is that those small purchases that cost only a few dollars (like a $5 latte at Starbucks) might not seem like much, but there is a compounding effect when totaled over time. If you do the math, you'll find that just $5 per day on lattes adds up to over $1,500 over the course of a year.

We all have our own personal "lattes" – it could be a cup of coffee and the newspaper you buy at the local convenience store each morning, or the protein bar you eat at the gym, or the quick lunch you buy every day at work. We're not saying you must completely cut out all these expenditures, but it makes sense to occasionally find a lower-cost alternative to replace a higher-cost habit.

For example, if you're someone who "needs" that super expensive coffee, then it might make sense to splurge on an espresso machine and brew coffee at home. Even if this machine is a few hundred dollars, you'll save that amount in a few short months by avoiding the cumulative effect of those small, $5 daily purchases.

Rebecca's financial advisor told her a story about a guy who liked to treat the neighborhood kids to ice cream at Baskin-Robbins. When he evaluated his spending, he found that he spent over $300 per month on just ice cream! He ditched the Baskin-Robbins trips and instead bought ice cream and toppings at the

---

105   https://www.amazon.com/Automatic-Millionaire-Expanded-Updated -Powerful-ebook/dp/B01G0GD0PE

grocery store. Rather than taking kids out for ice cream, he had them come to his place instead.

Finally, if your "latte factor" involves eating out, here are three simple strategies that can help:

1. Pack your lunch. One of the biggest culprits of the latte factor is fast food and takeout that many people grab for lunch during the workweek. You can minimize this expenditure by packing a lunch three to four times a week and letting the takeout lunch be a special weekly treat.

Packing your lunch doesn't mean you have to eat cold cut sandwiches or the same boring thing every day. You can add a lot of variety by planning lunches, or as Steve's wife does, packing dinner leftovers.

2. Use the Seated app. While eating at home saves a lot compared to eating out, there are times when a dinner out is a nice change of pace. Use Seated[106] when making reservations and you'll earn gift cards ranging in value from $10–$50.

3. Host dinner with friends. Dinner with drinks out with friends and family can be extremely expensive. In some places, you can easily drop $50 per person just for dinner and one or two drinks.

Obviously, it's important to maintain relationships, but you can get the same result by hosting an event on a rotating basis with the closest people in your life.

If you rotate, nobody feels the burden of hosting all the time. If someone enjoys hosting and has the room to have everyone over, do it potluck-style so the cost is spread out between all the participants.

---

106   https://www.seatedapp.io/

Rebecca was once part of a group that had dinner together twice a month. The host planned the theme (such as Mexican), and everyone signed up ahead of time to bring various menu items, ensuring they always had a delicious dinner with food that worked well together.

Okay, now that you know how to save money at mealtime, let's move on to the fifth and final money lever.

MONEY LEVER 5:

LIFE EXPENSES

Why This Money Lever?

While we've chosen to focus primarily on big financial wins, sometimes it's those small wins that can make a huge difference in your overall financial picture. This is especially true if you want to speed up getting out of debt, maxing out your retirement accounts, or saving for a large purchase such as a home. Every dollar you save moves you closer to your goals.

That's why with this final money lever, we have included a large assortment of simple ideas that can help stack your savings.

Apply to a Student Loan Forgiveness Program

A survey published by Consumer Federation of America[107] found that at the end of 2016, 42.4 million Americans owed $1.3 trillion in student loans. Even worse, the study found that an average of 3,000 people defaulted on their loans each day. To complicate this matter, student loan debt is one of the only types of personal credit that can't be discharged in a bankruptcy. The bottom line is that if you want to pay this money back, you need to figure out the most economical way to do so.

One way to do get rid of this debt is to apply for what's called *student loan forgiveness.*

The idea here is to work for a qualified federal, state, local, or charity organization for a set amount of time. Once you hit the necessary amount of time, you can apply to have your loan forgiven.

Since student loans are often one of the largest types of debt, applying for one of these types of jobs can help you shortcut a significant part of what you owe. On the other hand, you will have to work at a specific job for multiple years, so this decision shouldn't be taken lightly.

That's why we urge you to spend as much time as possible learning about how these various programs work. Here are two great articles that provide a detailed overview of student loan forgiveness.

---

107   https://consumerfed.org/press_release/new-data-1-1-million-federal-student-loan-defaults-2016/

- https://thecollegeinvestor.com/578/ways-to-get-student
  -loan-forgiveness/

- https://www.nerdwallet.com/blog/loans/student-loans/st
  udent-loan-forgiveness/

Also, you should consider refinancing these loans through a company like SoFi.[108] This company offers various types of refinancing loans, including student-loan refinancing. Since student loan rates constantly change, it might make sense to refinance if it means you'll pay a lower rate. However, like refinancing a mortgage, be sure to crunch the numbers to see if it's worth changing to a new loan.

---

108   https://www.sofi.com/refinance-student-loan/

Cut Your Financial Advisor Fee

If you use a financial advisor, you may pay as much as 1%–2% of your portfolio for assets under their management. To find out how much you're actually paying for financial advice in your investment accounts, you can use a service like FeeX,[109] which links to your investment accounts such as your 401(k) and analyzes what you are paying for fees and costs associated with them.

On the surface, these percentage points don't seem like much, but over a few decades you will start to see a noticeable difference. (The nerdwallet article, "How a 1% Fee Could Cost Millennials $590,000 in Retirement Savings"[110] explains the impact of giving away just a few percentage points to a financial advisor.)

The simple truth is a large number of financial advisors are salespeople who are financially incentivized to put you into mutual funds that generate the largest sales commission *for them*.

Rebecca learned this the hard way when she transitioned from a regular job to self-employment and rolled over her 401(k) into a new account recommended by a financial advisor. She wondered why her investments all of a sudden did so poorly. At the time, she didn't know much about investing, so she didn't take any action. Since then, she's taken control of her own retirement account with much better results.

If you ever need good financial advice (without the permanent

---

109 https://www.feex.com/

110 https://www.nerdwallet.com/blog/investing/millennial-retirement-fees
-one-percent-half-million-savings-impact/

percentage taken off your portfolio), consider hiring someone from The National Association of Personal Financial Advisors.[111] Here you will find an advisor who works on a fee basis instead of a sales commission. This is similar to hiring a CPA or attorney who you pay for *advice*, not to have them manage your finances.

And finally, nowadays it's pretty simple to put your money into index funds instead of even hiring a financial advisor in the first place. In fact, you can use the websites that we mentioned before to get an equal (or even better) return:

- Betterment[112] : Steve uses this for his emergency fund.

- Wealth Front[113] : Another robo-advisor, similar to Betterment.

- Stash[114] : Rebecca uses this for both an investment account and Roth IRA.

- Vanguard[115]: Steve uses this for his SEP IRA and long-term growth, investing specifically in VTSAX.[116] Rebecca has a Vanguard Roth IRA. In additional to individual stocks, she invests in VTSAX, which is also available as the ETF VTI, the Vanguard Total Bond Market BND,[117] and for international exposure, she puts a smaller amount in the Vanguard Total International Stock ETF, VXUS.[118] If you pick just one investment, VTSAX/VTI is a sound option.

---

111   https://www.napfa.org/

112   https://www.betterment.com/

113   https://www.wealthfront.com/

114   https://app.stashinvest.com/

115   https://investor.vanguard.com/home/

116   https://investor.vanguard.com/mutual-funds/profile/VTSAX

117   https://investor.vanguard.com/etf/profile/BND

118   https://investor.vanguard.com/etf/profile/VXUS

Learn How to Negotiate

The fine art of negotiation is one of the most important money-saving skills. If you know how to talk to people, you can simplify many of the strategies we cover in this book.

Negotiation helps in a variety of areas, such as increasing your salary, getting better deals, and asking for service charges to be waived. Rebecca and her husband considered going with a different Internet company, and before making the switch, her husband called their current company to let them know. Not wanting to lose their business, the company agreed to cut their Internet bill in half for two years.

If you need to brush up on your negotiating skills, be sure to check out the book *Never Split the Difference*[119] by former FBI hostage negotiator Chris Voss.

---

119   https://www.amazon.com/Never-Split-Difference-Negotiating-Depen
ded-ebook/dp/B014DUR7L2

Comparison Shop for Large-Ticket Items

Before making major purchases, it pays to comparison shop. *Consumer Reports*[120] is one of the best options for unbiased product reviews. *Consumer Reports* requires you to subscribe, or you can go to your local library to check out back issues.

Consumer Reports reviews a multitude of items such as:

- Appliances, including large appliances such as refrigerators, stoves, and dishwashers all the way down to small appliances such as coffee makers, slow cookers, and space heaters
- Items for babies and kids such as car seats, cribs, and bike helmets
- Car ratings for new and used cars, as well as car parts such as batteries and tires
- Electronics ranging from computers, smartphones, and cameras to antivirus software and headphones
- Health and personal care items such as blood pressure monitors, fitness trackers, and electric razors
- Items for the home such as mattresses, countertops, and toilets
- Garden items such as leaf blowers, grills, and lawnmowers
- Financial items such as banks, credit cards, and insurance

While there is a cost to *Consumer Reports*, if the subscription helps you make a wise decision on even one major purchase, it's worthwhile.

---

120   https://www.consumerreports.org

Invest in Quality over Quantity

Buying cheap products is one of the biggest mistakes people make when it comes to trying to save money. In the long run, buying cheap items often costs more than buying quality items since you'll likely have to replace cheaper items more frequently.

In addition to that, cheap items seldom bring joy in the same way as quality products do. Perhaps you've experienced frustration when you used a cheap item such as a bargain kitchen appliance that doesn't work well, and because of that you seldom use it, or if you do, it ends up breaking after minimal use.

One important lesson we've learned is to think of your purchases as investments. If you know you'll use an item frequently or use it for many years, it makes sense to buy the best, most durable option. This can include clothes, electronics, food, furniture, and appliances.

As an example, remember back when we talked about the latte factor and how those small, $5 coffee purchases can really add up over time? Well, if you purchased a high-end coffee maker, then you can potentially save over $100 per month (once you finished paying for this item).

You can also apply this logic to larger-ticket items like your home and car. (For more on this, check out the Lifehacker article, "When It Makes Sense to Buy Quality Instead of Saving Money."[121])

Finally, another way to keep from buying things simply because

---

121 http://lifehacker.com/when-it-makes-sense-to-buy-quality-instead-of-sa ving-mo-1689373996

they're on sale or cheap is to ask yourself, "Does this item spark joy?"

This concept was popularized by decluttering expert, Marie Kondo.[122] Her basic approach to decluttering is to one-by-one pick up each item in your home and ask yourself if it brings you joy. If it doesn't, it goes into the throw-away or give-away piles. If you use this approach, you'll have fewer possessions, but you'll use and love what you have.

You can apply this same concept to purchasing items.

For example, if you're in a clothing store and try something on and like it, but don't love it, realize that you will never like it more than you do in the store. If it doesn't bring you joy, walk away from it regardless of whether or not it's a "good deal."

---

122 https://konmari.com/

Kill Those Unnecessary Fees

One excellent habit to build is to examine all your expenses each month and kill any unnecessary fees. This requires you to go over each of your monthly bills and look for small items you frequently spend money on. This matters because when you consider the compounding effect of even a $5 recurring fee, these small fees really add up.

Here are a few examples:

- Late fees on rent
- ATM fees (for not using the bank's card)
- Bank fees
- Credit card yearly subscriptions
- DVR Rental for cable

Most, if not all, of these fees can be eliminated with just a small amount of thought and planning.

For example, if you regularly pay late fees for rent, focus on proper budgeting and put a reminder on your calendar to pay your rent on time—that should completely eliminate the fee. Budgeting also helps with ATM fees, since it eliminates unplanned withdrawals from ATM machines.

When it comes to bank fees, be sure you understand the terms of the account, and adjust your habits accordingly.

For instance, Rebecca and her husband are charged a $3.95 fee each month they don't use their checking account enough. One minor tweak they made to eliminate that fee was to break their monthly contribution to their church into four separate parts and pay it weekly instead of monthly. When it comes to annual credit card fees, ask yourself if you really need to spend upward of $100 for the privilege of using their card. If you have multiple cards with fees, get rid of all but one of them.

Find Unclaimed Payments and Property

Who doesn't love finding out they're owed money and that all they have to do is fill out a simple online form to be paid? We agree that on the surface this looks like a total scam, but it's true that businesses, organizations, and even state governments owe many people money. Sometimes the amount owed is small; other times it's more significant. Here are a few personal examples:

- Google paid Rebecca approximately $85.
- A former part-time job paid Rebecca $14.77.
- Rebecca's daughter received approximately $275 from a part-time job she worked as a teenager.
- Rebecca's son is owed more than $100 from a part-time job he worked in high school.
- Rebecca's sister-in-law is owed more than $100 from a state department of revenue.
- Steve got back $185 from the various companies that owed him money from the many moves he's had to make.

Check out these two sites for more information:

- Unclaimed[123]
- Missing Money[124]

---

123   https://www.unclaimed.org
124   https://www.missingmoney.com/Main/Search.cfm

Sell Your Car

While it may sound far-fetched to live without a car, in some areas and in some circumstances, it may make sense. After all, cars are only one way to get around.

As Steve's dad once eloquently put it when he asked for a ride somewhere as a kid: "What are those two things sticking out of your butt?"

Yes, indeed, if you're physically able and if you live in an area within walking- or biking-distance to places you want or need to go such as shops, restaurants, and businesses, walking or riding a bike is an option.

You may also opt to live without a car if you have good public transportation in your area. Three years ago, Rebecca and her husband decided to go carless. This move made sense for them since they are empty nesters, work from home, and live close to a train station. As an added bonus, they get more exercise since they do a lot of walking. In the three years they've been carless, they rented a car once for an out-of-town trip and used Uber or Lyft a dozen or so times. On occasion they catch a ride with friends or family members, but for the most part, walking, using public transportation, and online shopping make it easy for them to live without a car.

With no car, you can save on:

- Car insurance
- Gas
- Tolls
- Car loan payments

Since going carless is a drastic move for most people, there are many things to consider before making such a big lifestyle change.

Before you go carless, do the following:

1. Write down everything you currently do, and ask yourself how you'll do it without a car. For example, you likely now use your car when you go grocery shopping, so you'll need to figure out how to do that without a car. Before going carless, Rebecca tested out grocery delivery services and checked out bus and train routes to grocery stores. She then did test runs using public transportation combined with carrying groceries in a backpack to see if that option was realistic.

2. Consider the amount of time public transportation, walking, or biking takes compared to driving. While going carless definitely saves money, it will cost you in terms of time. For example, Rebecca and her husband could drive to their church in less than five minutes, and it takes them close to 15 minutes to walk. They don't mind this, as they get in some exercise, walk through a beautiful park, and enjoy the time to talk as they walk. While there are benefits to a calmer, slower pace of life, you do need to count the time cost of living without a car.

3. Consider what you'll cut out of your life as a result of going carless. Before making a commitment, Rebecca now goes on maps.google.com to check out bus or train routes. There are times when something is difficult to get to via public transportation, and unless she feels it's worth calling Uber or Lyft to get there, she chooses not to participate in the particular event. You could say she's missing out on a lot, but she enjoys committing only to things that are worth the effort.

4. Test out going carless while you still have a car. For at least a month before making the final decision to go carless, test out living without a car. Even though your car is sitting in your driveway, has insurance, and has gas in the tank, don't drive. Rebecca and her husband did this for three months. During those three months, they drove three times; each time, they drove just because they could, not because it was required. This gave them confidence that living without a car was 100% doable.

Buy a Used Car

Let's be honest, selling your car probably isn't an option for most people. But that doesn't mean that you have to pay top dollar for a car. One of the biggest ways to save money on a car is to buy a used car. According to Carfax.com,[125] new cars depreciate more than 20% after the first 12 months.

Check out the following used car resources:

Use *Consumer Reports*[126] to do research on cars that are one to three years old. Find the ones that you like, and then use the following sites to locate a car that's right for you:

- CarMax[127]
- Carfax[128]
- Kelly Blue Book[129]
- Edmunds[130]

Here are a few additional ways to save money on your car:

- Instead of going completely carless, cut back from two cars to one.
- Refinance[131] your car loan.
- Use public transportation some of the time.

---

125   https://www.carfax.com/blog/car-depreciation
126   https://www.consumerreports.org/cro/index.htm
127   https://www.carmax.com/
128   https://www.carfax.com
129   https://www.kbb.com/
130   https://www.edmunds.com/
131   https://www.nerdwallet.com/refinancing-auto-loans

- Clean up your driving record, and then contact your car insurance company to see if they'll lower your rates.

- Drive less aggressively and reduce your fuel consumption by up to 35%.[132]

- Perform regular maintenance such as tune-ups.

- Use Nextdoor[133] to find a good mechanic.

---

132 https://www.edmunds.com/fuel-economy/survival-strategies-for-steeper -gas-prices.html

133 https://nextdoor.com/join/

Buy "Lightly Used" Items

In addition to used cars, there are many other items you can buy used. There are so many items that are "like new" that it makes no sense to buy everything new. The key to all of this is to keep an ongoing list of things you think you might need in the future, and then keep an eye out for those items.

Think back to earlier in the book where Steve talked about his wife, Kristin, and her system for buying "like-new" clothing for their son. Kristin is part of multiple Facebook groups where local parents sell "bags of clothes" for $10–$20. So their son is usually dressed well (or as well as a rambunctious three-year-old can be) for a fraction of the cost that most parents spend on dressing their kids.

If you'd also like to save money on lightly used items, here are a few resources that can help you get started:

- Facebook Groups (just search for your town or county and a modifier like "stuff for sale")
- Craigslist[134]
- Garage / Yard Sales
- Freecycle,[135] which is a great network of people who trade goods in your local community
- thredUP,[136] an online consignment shop for women and children's clothing

---

134   https://www.craigslist.org/
135   https://www.freecycle.org
136   https://www.thredup.com/

- Swap.com[137]

- Nextdoor,[138] a social network for people who live in your neighborhood

Before you get too excited and start buying everything used, be sure to check out The Simple Dollar article "10 Things You Should Never Buy Used,"[139] for a clear explanation of why you should <u>never</u> buy the following items used:

- Baby cribs

- Car seats

- Mattresses

- Vacuum cleaners

- Makeup

- Shoes

- Baby bottles

- Worn cookware

- Upholstered furniture

- Hats

---

137   https://www.swap.com

138   https://nextdoor.com/join/

139   https://www.thesimpledollar.com/10-things-you-should-never-buy-used/

Pick the Right Time to Buy Items

In case you haven't noticed, there are certain times of year when various things are cheaper.

For instance, mattress stores often have Memorial Day sales, and you're more likely to get a good deal on appliances between September and November. If you know you need to buy something, plan ahead, pick the best time to do it, and then save up for the item to avoid going into debt. Check out the Lifehacker article "The Best Time to Buy Anything During the Year"[140] and the Nerdwallet article "What to Buy Every Month of the Year in 2019"[141] for lists of when to purchase everything from clothing to cruises to gym memberships and more.

---

140   https://lifehacker.com/5973864/the-best-time-to-buy-anything-during -the-year
141   https://www.nerdwallet.com/blog/shopping/what-to-buy-every-month/

Use Money-Saving Apps and Websites

Throughout this book we've shared a variety of tools that can help you save money. But here is a list of ten apps that can be invaluable while building the stack your savings habit.

1. Drop[142] may be the app for you if you're a "rewards point" chaser (and like simplicity). Through the app, members simply link their debit and credit cards to automatically earn points—eliminating the need to scan receipts, enter promo codes, or sign up for additional loyalty programs.

2. Acorns[143] is dedicated to helping save your "spare change" and turning it into a worthwhile investment. The Acorns Core account takes generally less than five minutes to set up and will automatically add money to your diversified portfolio, built with help from a Nobel laureate. And the Acorns Later account is where the company recommends an IRA that's right for you and updates it regularly to match your goals. Finally, the Acorns Spend account is a debit card that puts your checking account to work for you.

3. Ibotta[144] allows users to earn cash back on items they purchase regularly. Things like milk, eggs, bread, butter, cheese, razors, toothpaste, toilet paper ... even liquor. Ibotta also offers discounts (typically ranging from 2–5% back) for shopping online at their partner stores. Similar to Drop, once you sign up for an Ibotta account, it will ask you to select your favorites from a list of supported retailers— both brick-and-mortar and online.

---

142   https://www.earnwithdrop.com/
143   https://www.acorns.com/
144   https://ibotta.com/

4. Digit[145] analyzes your spending and automatically saves the perfect amount every day so you don't have to worry. All you need to do is share some basic information, such as what you're saving for (rainy-day fund, goals, bills), and Digit does the rest. If the app is able to find money, Digit will auto-transfer those savings to your Digit account.

5. Honey[146] prides itself on doing the work for you when it comes to searching for coupon codes. You can simply add the "honey" button to your chrome browser and let the app take care of the rest. And with just one simple click of the "honey" button during checkout, the app will automatically apply the best coupon codes to your shopping cart at over 10,000 stores. Honey also partners with Amazon[147] to discover the best time to buy, with price history charts and alerts for when your favorite products go on sale. There is even a "trending" section with the day's hottest deals.

6. Trim[148] focuses on helping users "trim" their spending by tracking their expenses. Simply input a bit of information and Trim will help you: cancel unwanted subscriptions, monitor your utility bills, negotiate cable rates, track your spending, and transfer the money you save into a high-yield account.

7. RetailMeNot[149] is an app that allows you to search and upload scannable coupons on your phone in seconds. Not your typical coupon search, the app offers trending deals and big savings—including cash back and gift card discount

145   https://digit.co/
146   https://www.joinhoney.com/
147   https://www.amazon.com/
148   https://www.developgoodhabits.com/trim
149   https://www.retailmenot.com/

offers from their partners. All one needs to do is click on the offer to accept it.

8. Paribus[150] is like having a retail lawyer on retainer, and it's 100% free to join! Basically it monitors popular online merchants and travel websites, such as:

- Target
- Nordstrom
- Walmart
- Gap
- Macy's
- Expedia
- Priceline
- Hotels.com
- Booking.com
- Marriott

Then, once users make their purchase, Paribus checks for potential savings or refund opportunities based on purchase history. Simply put: **when a price drops after you buy (within the time allowed in the merchant's price drop policy), Paribus helps you get a refund for the difference.**

9. Chime[151] is an online-only bank that believes they offer "Banking the way it should be." When you open a savings account with Chime, the free mobile banking platform allows you to benefit from microsavings and rewards features every time you use the Chime debit card with their Automatic Savings feature. Saving money is a snap with the

---

150   https://www.developgoodhabits.com/paribus
151   https://www.chimebank.com/

"Round Up" feature that puts extra change in your account with every purchase. For example, if you spend $6.36 on a sandwich for lunch, Round Up will automatically fund your savings account with 64 cents.

10. Camel Camel Camel[152] is for the Amazon junkie. They offer a free Amazon price tracker that monitors millions of products and alerts you when prices drop, helping you decide when to buy. Simply sign up and link your Amazon.com account to get started. From that moment on, the Camel price tracker monitors the prices of about six million Amazon products across different countries (primarily throughout the United States and the United Kingdom).

---

152   https://camelcamelcamel.com/

Reduce Your Cell Phone Bill

It's not at all uncommon for people to spend the ridiculous price of over $100 per month on just their cell phone. Here are a few ways to spend less on your cell phone bill:

Consider how you use a cell phone and purchase just what you need. For instance, Rebecca's mom only uses her cell phone to make phone calls, so she doesn't need a smartphone or a data plan. If you only use your cell phone for occasional calls when you're away from home, opt for a prepaid phone.

For instance, Tracfone's[153] cheapest plan is $9.99 per month, with any combination of 30 minutes of talk and texts. Ting[154] has flexible plans based on the number of lines you want, the amount of talk time, texting, and data. At the current time it runs $9 per month for one line with 100 minutes of talk time. If you want to add on 100 texts, it runs $12 per month, and if you add on 100 MB of data, the cost is $15 per month. Obviously, each of these options work best for those who use a cell phone occasionally.

Use a free online phone service. Google Voice[155] requires an existing phone number to work, but it's a great way to get a second phone number for free. There is also a Google Voice Chrome app that enables you to talk and send and receive messages via your computer.

Use a family plan, and split the cost. As an example, Rebecca and her husband, daughter, son, and son-in-law are all on the

---

153   https://www.tracfone.com/shop/plans
154   https://ting.com/rates
155   https://voice.google.com/u/0/signup

same plan. Each member of the family has unlimited data and talk time and pays a total of around $135 per month, or $27 per month per phone.

Use Wi-Fi instead of data. Since Wi-Fi is readily available both at home and in most public places, save money on data charges by using Wi-Fi. Republic Wireless[156] has low-cost options focused on Wi-Fi and allows you to buy one GB of high-speed LTE data at a time on an as-needed basis.

If you want to get rid of your cell phone bill completely, give FreedomPop[157] a try. FreedomPop's basic plan is free and includes 200 minutes of voice, 500 texts, and 200MB data. Note that if you heavily rely on your phone for business or personal use, it may be inadvisable to use a free option such as FreedomPop.

Buy new phones less frequently. Some phone plans provide a new phone every two years. While it's nice, the new phone isn't really free, as it's figured into the price of your cell phone contract. Check to see if you can get a contract that doesn't include the "free" phone and then wait as long as possible before buying a new phone. At some point, you'll likely find that newer apps won't work with your older phone and may decide to upgrade at that time.

For instance, Steve still uses his iPhone 5 that he purchased over five years ago. It's a bit buggy and doesn't have the new features like other phones, but it still works for him!

---

156   https://republicwireless.com
157   https://www.freedompop.com/

Focus on Needs Not Wants

Sometimes even the most frugal people succumb to a consumerist mentality. This mentality convinces you that you NEED something, when the reality is you simply want it but could easily live without it.

For instance, if you love kitchen gadgets, and love quesadillas, when you see a quesadilla maker in a store or online, you may feel that you need it. You may even convince yourself that it will save you money since you can make quesadillas at home instead of buying them in restaurants. While it's true that making food at home saves money, since you only need either a skillet or a microwave to make quesadillas at home, the quesadilla maker is not a need but a want.

There are two key questions to ask yourself before making purchases:

1. Is this a need or a want?
2. Can I already _____ (e.g., make quesadillas) without _____ (e.g., the quesadilla maker)?

Many times, you'll find the answers to the questions lead you to removing the item from your shopping cart. Other times, you may determine it truly is a need or at the very least is something that will save you money. If you tend to buy espresso every day on the way to work, buying an espresso machine is an example of a want that saves money since you do need special equipment to make espresso, and making it at home is cheaper than buying it out.

By the way, it's especially important to focus on needs versus wants when things are on sale. Just because something is on sale doesn't mean it's a good deal if it's something you really don't need.

Another thing you might want to consider is to create a "pause" before making major purchases. And if you're married, include your spouse in the process.

Many couples find it helpful to set a dollar limit they can spend without first discussing the purchase. Others find it helpful to wait 24 hours, 48 hours, or even a month before they pull the trigger and buy a big-ticket item. Steve prefers to use the **72-hour rule**, as discussed by the Frugalwoods on their blog.[158]

---

158 https://www.frugalwoods.com/2017/01/09/my-foolproof-method-to-stop-impulse-spending/

Unsubscribe from Mailing Lists

Junk mail tempts people to buy stuff on impulse, instead of in response to actual needs. If you receive a never-ending stream of catalogs and coupons, you'll likely make unnecessary purchases. Sure, saving 20% on a purchase may seem like a good deal, but it's not a savings at all if you spend $100 to save $20. The reality is, you didn't save $20, you spent $80. Keep that in mind the next time you find a catalog or coupons that are full of "savings."

Removing temptation is an even better option than doing your best to resist temptation. The best way to do this is to eliminate unwanted mail.

The service Catalog Choice,[159] eliminates *most* unwanted mailings within about a month. You can then take the following steps to get off other unwanted lists.

- Go to DMACHOICE.org[160] to get rid of unwanted magazines and newsletters.

- If you're in the US, go to OptOutPrescreen.com[161] to get rid of unwanted credit card offers.

- Write to the mail preference service (for the US or the UK) to remove your name from the major mailing lists.

- Stop giving your address on surveys and raffles since your information will likely be sold to other companies.

- Every time you get an unwanted catalog or promotional item in the mail, ask the individual senders to remove you from their mailing list.

---

159   https://www.catalogchoice.org/
160   https://dmachoice.thedma.org/
161   https://www.optoutprescreen.com/

- Request to make your personal information confidential in the county and state database.
- Add a "No Junk Mail" or "No Free Papers" sign on your mailbox.
- Sign up to receive statements and bills electronically.

These steps require a lot of effort, but if you work at it a little every week or month, you'll drastically reduce the amount of junk mail you receive.

If you still receive junk mail after all this, quickly toss any unwanted catalogs or coupons without even browsing through them.

Take Advantage of Your Local Library

Libraries are a treasure trove of free or low-cost items. Unfortunately, not many people ever take the time to check out this amazing resource that's usually right down the road. If you're looking for an inexpensive way to entertain yourself (and your family), here are a few items that are usually available at your local library:

- An interlibrary loan program[162] is offered at most locations
- Children's books
- Various community programs
- Rentals on movies, magazines, audiobooks, CDs, etc.
- Software and apps
- Language-learning programs (like Rosetta Stone)
- Community programs
- Educational classes
- Concerts
- Recording studios complete with audio and video equipment
- Computers and other devices such as Kindles
- Book clubs
- Game nights
- Movies shown on a big screen (Rebecca's library even serves free popcorn and lemonade!)

---

162   https://en.wikipedia.org/wiki/Interlibrary_loan

- Subscriptions to e-learning sites such as Lynda.com and brain games sites such as BrainHQ[163]

- Some libraries even have art prints you can check out to hang up in your home

To quote Matt Damon's character from *Good Will Hunting* (one of Steve's favorite movies), "You wasted $150,000 on an education you coulda got for $1.50 in late fees at the public library."

It's true that especially with interlibrary loan you can learn just about anything from library books and other resources.

For instance, when Steve was researching real estate investing, after doing a Google search, he made a list of the best books on the subject. He tried borrowing them from his local library, but they didn't have most of the titles in stock. But since his library is part of the Bergen County, New Jersey, interlibrary system, he was able to request all of them from the dozens of neighboring locations—for free!

If you're interested in buying a book, see if you can check it out of the library. From there, evaluate whether the book adds enough value to make it part of your personal library.

If you spend a lot of time at the library and make a point of getting to know the librarians, they may even order books for you. Rebecca homeschooled when her children were young, and the library was their second home. As such, she developed a good relationship with the children's librarian, who more than once ordered a book to add to the library's collection at Rebecca's request. She even once ordered the ten-volume *A History of US* series so Rebecca could use it as their history curriculum. This

---

163   https://www.brainhq.com/?v4=true&fr=y

single special-request library order saved Rebecca over $200 in curriculum costs!

If you prefer electronic media, many libraries are part of the OverDrive system,[164] and some also participate in Hoopla Digital,[165] which provides eBooks, audiobooks, movies, TV shows, and music—all free of charge.

---

164 https://www.overdrive.com/account/sign-in
165 https://www.hoopladigital.com/

Entertain Your Children—On the Cheap

The great thing about kids is that, for the most part, you don't have to spend a lot of money to entertain them. They mostly want your time and attention. The younger they are, the easier it is to do free and inexpensive things. When Rebecca's kids were young, she could get away with allowing them to play arcade games—without putting any money in the machines. They also spent a lot of time at the Disney store in the mall, looking at the merchandise and watching the Disney movies playing on the big screen.

To really get the wheels turning, check out these ideas for ways to find fun events in your area:

- **Eventful.com**[166] does a great job aggregating events for those who live in or near a big city.

- **Local newspapers, magazines, and websites** feature activities for all ages.

- **Google** is great if you have an idea of something cool to try but don't know how to get started. Simply do a Google search for what you're interested in, together with the name of your city. For instance, when Rebecca did a Google search for "cheap indoor play areas in the Denver area" she came across an article, "Indoor Play Areas For Kids Around Denver,"[167] that includes a list of stores, malls, and restaurants with free play areas.

  If you don't have any bright ideas but want to find an inexpensive outing, a more generic search such as, "cheap

---

166   http://www.eventful.com/
167   https://www.milehighonthecheap.com/indoor-play-areas-kids-denver/

things to do in [your city]" may lead you to a site with a ton of options, such as Mile High on the Cheap,[168] a treasure trove of free and cheap things to do in the Denver area.

- **Map out a walking tour** or take advantage of planned walking tours your city offers. The Denver suburb where Rebecca lives offers free historical walking tours hosted by volunteers that are part of the historical preservation board. If your area doesn't have planned tours, involve the family in mapping out your own walking tour.

- **Only In Your State**[169] is a website with a massive collection of articles that feature interesting state-specific attractions.

- **Try geocaching,** an activity that provides GPS coordinates with a few clues that lead you to a hidden cache. This turns a simple walk into a treasure hunt! This activity is popular enough that Rebecca discovered more than 6,000 geocaches in her area through the Geochaching website.[170]

- **Bulletin board flyers** are a great place to find local events that may be too small to get much notice in the local paper. But if you keep an eye on bulletin boards around town, you'll discover a number of smaller local events that are worth checking out.

- **Craigslist**[171] is a useful resource to find listings for fun activities, interest-specific groups, volunteering opportunities, local events, and classes.

- **Meetup.com** is a great place to find groups based off your personal interests and make new friends as you enjoy one of your favorite activities.

---

168   https://www.milehighonthecheap.com/
169   http://www.onlyinyourstate.com/
170   https://www.geocaching.com/play
171   http://craigslist.org/

- **Annual memberships** can save money and help you to enjoy what your city has to offer. These aren't free, but if you take advantage of the memberships, they provide an inexpensive form of entertainment. When Rebecca's kids were young, she and her husband purchased annual memberships to places like the children's museum, zoo, aquarium, and art museum. Almost every week they took advantage of one of their memberships, and since they often packed a picnic lunch, the cost was minimal.

Cut the Cord

With all of the options for online entertainment, it's possible to lower your cable bill or even eliminate it completely.

Here is one option Steve has, which reduced his cable bill by $60 each month:

- Netflix
- Small package with Hulu (which also gives him access to the Spotify music service)
- Amazon Prime TV, which he already pays for with his regular Prime account

The total cost is $22 per month.

Rebecca cut her online entertainment cost by sharing accounts with her young-adult kids in a way that is totally legitimate. She and her husband pay for a Netflix account that allows up to four profiles, and up to two screens on at a time. She shared her login information with her adult children, and they set up their own profiles. Her daughter and son-in-law purchased a Hulu subscription, and they shared the login information with Rebecca and her husband. Similar to the Netflix arrangement, Hulu allows more than one profile and therefore is meant to be shared. Rebecca's cost for Netflix is $11.32 per month, including tax. Between Netflix and her free Hulu access, she has more than enough media to watch at a very low cost.

If you choose to stick with cable, you can decrease your bill by letting go of premium channels and other high-cost options such as DVR. It also never hurts to call the cable company to see if you can negotiate a lower rate.

Reduce Your Utility Bills

Turning off lights and unplugging appliances in your home or office not only saves money, it also helps the environment. For best results, add these tiny actions to your daily routine:

1. Turn off lights whenever you leave a room.

2. Power down electronics when they're not being used. (Many electronics will often go into "standby" mode that still uses some electricity.) To eliminate phantom power, unplug anything not in use unless unplugging them messes up things such as clocks or other important settings.

3. Open windows and use fans for cooling in the summertime, saving the air conditioning for those oppressively hot days. If you have old windows, replace them with energy-efficient windows. This is costly upfront, but will make you more comfortable and will save on heating and cooling costs in the long run.

4. Open the blinds and shades in the winter, which lets the sunshine in and warms your home without expending additional energy.

5. Match your pot size to the properly sized burner. Using a small pot or pan on a larger electric coil means you expend more energy to get the same result.

6. Use cold water to do loads of laundry. The results are nearly as good, but it costs about 40 cents less per load of laundry than washing clothes with hot water. Using cold water also increases the lifespan of many clothing items.

7. Turn off the water heater if you are going to leave your home for a few days. It takes an hour to get a water heater

to reheat the water and saves quite a bit of energy over the days you are gone.

8. Stop your dryer when lightweight, hangable clothes are still damp. Hang them up immediately, and they'll air dry and be wrinkle-free.

9. Make sure your home is properly insulated, and air seal[172] it by caulking and weatherstripping.

---

172 https://www.energy.gov/energysaver/weatherize/air-sealing-your-home

Reduce Your "Gift-Giving" Costs

We'll admit that having a conversation about gift-giving with those you love can be tough and uncomfortable, but it's worthwhile if you feel that gift-giving is getting out of control. In spite of the initial discomfort, you may find that people are relieved when you agree to a hug and a handshake instead of gifts.

Steve and his wife have a basic agreement to focus on experiences rather than gifts. Since neither Rebecca nor her husband care too much about gifts, except for rare occasions, they've focused Christmas gift-giving on their kids rather than each other. They've also cut down on gift-giving expectations.

For instance, since Rebecca's birthday is two days before Valentine's Day, they celebrate both occasions at the same time with a single dinner out and then a birthday cake at home.

For the kids, rather than spending a ton of money on gifts, invest in their 529 college savings plan or add money to their bank account or piggy bank.

Homemade gifts are another great option. Pinterest is chock-full of homemade gift ideas, and the article "Homemade Gifts"[173] on The Simple Dollar provides inspiration and links to instruction for everything from homemade beer to homemade soaps and meals in jars.

One of the easiest, lowest-cost ideas is to make coupon books for acts of service. Rebecca's daughter was low on cash one

---

173 https://www.thesimpledollar.com/homemade-gift-series-wrap-up-both-li
terally-and-otherwise/

Christmas, and because of that, she chose to make her a coupon book for pampering services such as facials. Since Rebecca doesn't care too much for material things but loves being pampered, to this day that is her favorite gift from her daughter.

Reduce Your Vacation "Food Bill"

Meals consume (pun intended) a large part of vacation expenses, especially if you have little ones. The good news is, there are lots of ways to trim the fat.

When Rebecca was growing up, her family couldn't afford fancy vacations, but they went camping often. Her parents hitched up a small cargo trailer to the family station wagon, and her mom used the regular grocery budget to pack it with food. Rebecca has fond memories of keeping a gallon of milk cold in an icy stream and savoring the delicious taste of pancakes and bacon cooked outdoors.

If camping is not your thing, you can still save a lot on meals by staying in a hotel that provides a full breakfast, or an Airbnb that serves breakfast or provides kitchen facilities. If you're driving to a vacation destination, plan ahead and pack a cooler[174] with food, pans, spices, and so on. This isn't to say that you can't eat out at all when on vacation. Rebecca found that she and her family need one hot meal a day to feel satisfied, so they typically eat out of the cooler twice a day and enjoy a leisurely hot restaurant meal each day when traveling.

---

174 https://www.amazon.com/Arctic-Zone-Blend-Thermal-Tote/dp/B00314 DM6Q/

Lastly ...

This last suggestion is a simple one in practice, but it's hard to do consistently:

Get into the habit of looking at every expenditure in your life each month **and ask yourself, "Is this expenditure more important than my short-term and long-term goals?"**

If it isn't, do all you can to eliminate or minimize it.

Remember, this entire book is about finding those big levers in your life and looking for ways to cut corners so you'll end up with big savings over the long run. By reviewing your expenditures once a month, you'll start to strip away those small spending habits that eat into your ability to fulfill many of your short- and long-term goals.

HOW TO BUILD THE STACK
YOUR SAVINGS HABIT

As you've seen, we've covered a lot of ideas up to this point. From one-time actions that can quickly reduce your monthly bills to full lifestyle changes that will take deliberate planning, we've talked about a variety of topics that can help you save money.

So, the question you might have is: "How do I get started?"

Well, in this section we'll show you how to turn *information into action*. Specifically, we're going to talk about the process for incorporating the stack your savings framework into your life. What you're about to learn is the nine-step process that Steve personally uses to build *any* habit. But *you* will use it to start making those small, but important, financial decisions that will positively impact your life.

STEP 1: Connect Saving Money to Your Purpose

If you try to save money just because you think you should or because you feel pressured to do so by friends or family, you'll likely fail. To increase the odds of your success, it's important to attach the money-saving habit to a reason that deeply resonates with you. Connecting with your purpose will help you stick with your money-saving goals when things get tough.

Discover Your Underlying Reason

The first step in this process is to connect with the underlying reason of why you'd like to build the money-saving habit.

Earlier, in Pillar 4, Steve shared that his purpose for saving up for a 20% down payment on rental properties is so that he won't have to pay PMI, and Rebecca shared that the thing that motivates her to save as much as possible toward retirement is because if her husband passes away before she does, without working hard on this goal, she'll face hard financial times in her retirement years.

We all have our different reasons for wanting to save money. But let's dig deeper into *why* saving in every aspect of life toward retirement matters:

- Social security may become a thing of the past, and even if it doesn't, it was never meant to cover all expenses.

- You want to avoid being a financial burden on your children and other family members who may have to support you financially if you fail to save.

- Your children may not be willing or able to support you financially, and you certainly don't want to be homeless or have to eat dog food when you're retired.
- You don't want to have to work until the day you die.
- You want to leave an inheritance to your children and grandchildren.
- You dream of traveling the world during your golden years and won't be able to do so if you fail to save for retirement.

Consider Your Biggest Financial Pain Points

One of the best ways to connect with your why for building the money-saving habit is to recognize the pain that not having this habit brings. Consider both your past experiences as well as the future pain you'll endure (e.g., eating dog food in retirement) if you don't develop the money-saving habit.

Here are some example questions to ask yourself:

- What are the worst things that have happened to me as a result of not saving money?
- Do I have any financial regrets due to not saving money in the past?
- How has not saving money impacted my loved ones in the past, and how will it impact them in the future?
- What bad spending habits do I want to break?
- What excuses have I made when it comes to any money-saving failures?

Again: There isn't a wrong answer to any of these questions. The goal of this exercise is to identify the specific mental blocks that *you* currently experience when it comes to saving money.

Your Version of Financial Freedom

Before we go further, we want to make it clear that there is no right or wrong reason for developing the money-saving habit. The key is to determine how you define financial freedom and how saving money fits with that definition.

As an example, Steve likes to travel with his family, so saving money in other areas of life provides money that gives them the freedom to enjoy amazing (but surprisingly affordable) trips.

For Rebecca, freedom to work part-time from home motivates her to save money in other areas of life so that she doesn't get stuck working a regular job.

We hope these examples illustrate that as you consider your deeper purpose, it's important to let go of the "shoulds" and embrace what truly matters most to you.

Keep this purpose in mind whenever you feel the urge to spend money. Ask yourself, "Does this expenditure align with my short- and long-term goals?"

YOUR ACTION PLAN

Remember, if you try to build the money-saving habit just because you think you should, you'll likely fail, so take the time to dig deeper into why saving money matters to you and how it will impact not just you but other members of your family as well.

To get started, buy a journal and then answer these reflection questions:

- What's the #1 reason you want to develop the money-saving habit? Is it because you're tired of looking at an empty bank account? Is it because you don't want to be a financial burden to your kids in your old age or because you want to be able to put your kids through college debt-free?
- What does financial freedom look like to you?
- How has your failure to save money in the past impacted you and those you love?
- What impact will saving money have on both your present and future?
- How far are you willing to go to make your financial dreams a reality?

If you choose to write about the positive impacts of saving money, write as if your future hope is a present reality. Doing so will bring positive money-related feelings to the surface and give you a more hopeful perspective on the topic of saving money.

STEP 2: Create Money-Saving S.M.A.R.T. Goals

Earlier in this book we talked about the following five money levers:

Lever 1: Credit cards and your credit score

Lever 2: Home ownership

Lever 3: Insurance

Lever 4: Meals

Lever 5: Life expenses

With these areas in mind, create a list of all your monthly and occasional expenditures and then identify the areas where you'll have the biggest savings.

As you create your money-saving goals, you'll focus on the areas with the biggest savings potential first. From there you'll work downward until you're focusing on small tweaks you can use to save a little bit of money.

Goals versus Habit

Goals and habits work together to help you fulfill your purpose, but they aren't the same thing. *Goals* are the broad outcomes, and *habits* are your day-to-day execution on the goals. You may get all fired up when you think about your goals and feel a bit bored by the idea of habits, but habits are what ultimately determine whether or not you accomplish your goals.

Create S.M.A.R.T. Money-Saving Goals

If you've read our book, *The Budgeting Habit*,[175] you're already familiar with the concept of S.M.A.R.T. goals. If you need a refresher, or if this is a new concept for you, read on for details on how to accomplish your financial dreams through S.M.A.R.T. goals.

To begin, let's start with a simple definition of S.M.A.R.T. goals, an acronym first used by George Doran.

S.M.A.R.T. stands for:

- Specific;
- Measurable;
- Attainable;
- Relevant; and
- Time-bound.

Specific

Specific goals answer your six "W" questions:

- Who?
- What?
- When?
- Where?
- Which?
- Why?

---

175   https://www.amazon.com/Budgeting-Habit-Budget-Develop-Habits-ebook/dp/B07F8J6DKP

When you can identify each element, you'll know which tools (and actions) you require to reach a goal.

Specificity is necessary because if you're not specific, you'll never know when you reach your goal.

Measurable

Measurable goals are defined with precise times, amounts, or other units—essentially anything that measures progress toward a goal.

Generally, a measurable goal statement answers questions starting with *how*, such as:

- How much?
- How many?
- How fast?

Attainable

Attainable goals are possible but are often challenging and full of obstacles. To set an attainable goal, look at your current situation and set a goal that seems slightly beyond your reach.

Relevant

Relevant goals focus on what you truly desire. They fit with your purpose and are in harmony with everything that is important in your life.

Time-Bound

Time-bound goals have specific deadlines. You are expected to achieve your desired outcome before a target date. You can set your target date for today, or you can set it for a few months, a few weeks, or a few years from now. The key to creating a time-bound goal is to set a deadline you'll meet by working backward and developing habits (more on this later).

9 Examples of S.M.A.R.T. Money-Saving Goals

To briefly demonstrate this concept, here are nine S.M.A.R.T. goals related to the money-saving habit:

1. **Credit:** I will pay off my Chase Visa card by July 3rd of this year. I'll make a payment and review my progress on the 30th of each month.

2. **Meals:** I'll reduce my average food budget from $700 to $500 per month by creating a meal plan that focuses on items on sale at the grocery store. I'll complete meal planning each week no later than Friday night at 10:00 p.m. and grocery shop on the weekend.

3. **Life Expenses:** I will reduce my monthly spending on gasoline by 30% starting on May 1st by carpooling with my coworker, Debbie.

4. **Savings:** I will put $1,000 in an emergency fund by December 31. I'll add to my savings by depositing $100 per month from the money that I'll save as a result of bringing my lunch to work four days per week.

5. **Home Ownership:** I'll eliminate PMI by December 31st of next year by paying an additional $300 per month on my principle.

6. **Credit:** I'll raise my credit score from 590 to 700 by November 15 by following the tips in this book.

7. **Life Expenses:** By July 15th, I will decrease my cell phone bill from $75 per month to $25 per month by eliminating my data plan.

8. **Investing:** I will save 10% of every paycheck and invest it in index funds through Vanguard.

9. **Meals:** Beginning next month, rather than eating lunch out, I'll pack my lunch four days per week.

See how we listed specific goals? These goals are S.M.A.R.T. because there's no ambiguity—you'll know beyond a doubt whether or not you've reached each of your goals.

YOUR ACTION PLAN

At the beginning of this chapter we tasked you with writing down all of your expenses and identifying the areas with the biggest savings potential. If you haven't already done that, do it now.

List the top ten areas where you can save money. Spend ten minutes brainstorming ways you can save money on those ten areas.

After reviewing the S.M.A.R.T. goal components and our examples, refer back to the list of your top ten areas where you can save money, and write down between five and ten S.M.A.R.T. goals related to those items.

Don't worry—you don't need to work on all of these goals at once. In fact, we believe in starting small, so pick just one of your goals to start working on in the next 24 hours.

Finally, add a reminder to your calendar to check your weekly or monthly progress on your goal. When you near the completion of one goal, decide what goal to focus on next.

STEP 3: Turn Goals into Habits

In step 2, you created S.M.A.R.T. goals. In order to accomplish those goals, now is the time to turn those goals into habits, or a series of small habits. These habits are clear, identifiable actions that you'll complete every day, week, or month.

Different Types of Habits

There are three different categories of habit types:

- Yes or no: Did you complete this habit for the day?
- Metric-based: A certain time, amount, or quantity to reach your goal for the day.
- Project-based: Milestones where you chip away at a larger goal that has a multitude of steps. This is what Steve calls, "elephant habits" in his book *Habit Stacking: 127 Small Changes to Improve Your Health, Wealth, and Happiness*.[176]

You can also break these habits into how frequently you plan to do them. Some examples are daily, weekly, monthly, and quarterly. There are other things that you'll do just once.

Daily Habits

Daily habits are the foundation when it comes to taking small, manageable steps toward your goals. The trick is to ask yourself, "What can I do every day?"

---

176   https://www.developgoodhabits.com/hs2_amazon

Keep the following two things in mind as you set your daily habits.

1. Make sure your daily habits move you closer to accomplishing your goals.

2. Make sure they're realistic (the R in S.M.A.R.T.). If the goals you set require unrealistic daily habits, adapt the goals to be more realistic.

Here are a few daily money-saving habits:

- Review and log your expenditures from that day.
- Check your budget before spending any money.
- Open any bills that arrived via mail or email and schedule a reminder to pay them.
- Cook at least one meal.
- Review the recipe for tomorrow's meal(s) and move meat from the freezer to the fridge to thaw.
- Check your refrigerator for leftovers. Make a plan to use the leftovers before they go bad.
- Before spending money, ask yourself, "Is this a need or a want?"

Weekly, Monthly, and Quarterly Habits

In addition to your daily money-saving habits, plan to add a few weekly, monthly, or quarterly habits to your life. These habits matter and help you accomplish your financial goals but may be more time consuming and simply don't need to be done on a daily basis.

For example, Rebecca and her husband have a weekly budget meeting where they review their spending for the past week and make any needed adjustments to their budget. During this meeting, they move money around in their budgeting software if they've overspent in a category, allocate any income that's come in during the week, and make any necessary bank deposits. On a monthly basis they review all bank and investment account balances, review their house value and mortgage, and calculate their net worth. They then discuss their progress on their big-picture financial goals.

Another example is Steve's weekly habit of reviewing his credit card statements and paying bills. Not only does he look for inaccuracies in these expenses, Steve also identifies certain "spending leaks" that can be eliminated from his family's budget.

Here are a few weekly, monthly, and quarterly ideas to consider:

- Allocate funds to the appropriate budget categories on every payday.
- Evaluate your progress toward your S.M.A.R.T. financial goals.
- Check your credit card statements for recurring charges that you may be able to eliminate.
- Check the weekly grocery store flyer to identify any food items worth stocking up on.
- Plan your menu for the week.
- Shop for meal ingredients.
- Review your budget with your spouse.
- Review your investments and rebalance your portfolio if needed. (Be aware of any trading fees charged by your investment company, and do this step infrequently if there are fees.)

- Comparison shop for major items you'd like to purchase such as cars, appliances, and electronics.
- Evaluate your account balances, and if you have extra funds available, make an additional house payment or extra contribution to your IRA account.

One-Time Actions

In this book, we've covered many money-saving actions that you only need to do once. Here are some examples of one-time actions:

- Set up a 529 plan for each of your children.
- Sign up for your company's 401(k) and fill out any needed paperwork to get your contributions started.
- Start a Roth IRA and set up automatic contributions.
- Cancel cable and sign up for a lower-cost alternative such as Netflix.
- Switch to a cheaper cell phone plan.
- Refinance your mortgage.
- Set up automated payments to pay off your credit cards.
- Subscribe to a menu plan service.
- Move to a cheaper home.
- Cancel unnecessary credit cards that have an annual fee.
- Contact your Internet provider to negotiate a lower price.
- Invest in energy-efficient home improvements such as replacing windows and adding insulation.

There is a seemingly endless supply of daily, weekly, and monthly habits that can help you save money. The key is to identify the ones that will have the greatest impact on moving you closer to accomplishing your financial goals. Once you've done that, add those items to your schedule.

YOUR ACTION PLAN

Create a list of daily habit options that will move you closer to your money-saving goals. Rank these habits in order of priority. Commit to doing your top choices on a daily basis. Create phone or calendar alerts to remind you to do the habit each day.

Next, make a list of weekly, monthly, quarterly, and one-time habits you want to implement. Determine when you'll do them and add reminders to your calendar.

Write your daily, weekly, monthly, and quarterly habits along with answers to the reflection questions in your journal.

STEP 4: Build the Stack Your Savings Habit

To build the stack your savings habit, we'll use Steve's habit-stacking process. Basically, the way to do this is to create a daily or weekly routine that includes a small series of money-saving habits.

The basic components of habit-stacking are:

1. Identify small money-saving related items.
2. Group them together in a routine with equally important actions.
3. Schedule a time to complete the stack each day or week.
4. Use a trigger—something you already do consistently—to remind you to complete the stack.
5. Make it super easy to get started.

When creating a habit stack, consider the following:

- What's the purpose of each action?
- What's the most logical order?
- How much time will each activity require?

The key to effective habit stacking is to treat each habit stack like a single action, rather than a series of individual tasks. This makes things easier because a single action only needs to be scheduled once, requires just one trigger, and is only one thing to track. A habit stack makes it easier to remember and reduces overwhelm, and thus increases the odds that you'll do it consistently.

To better understand the habit-stacking concept, check out Steve's blog post "13 Steps for Building a Habit Stacking

Routine,"[177] which explains the step-by-step process of building a habit stack.

Now let's take a look at the six-step process for building a money-saving specific habit stack.

1. Focus on one habit stack at a time.

If you try to add too many new habits into your already busy life, you'll likely quit. Because of that, it's important to commit to just a few simple habits that only take five to ten minutes to complete.

Here's an example of a simple finance-related habit stack that includes daily habits we've discussed earlier:

- Review and log expenditures that you made during the day.
- Review your budget to check balances in each of your budget categories.
- If you overspent in any area, consider why the overspending occurred. Did you miscalculate how much money you needed, or did you purchase something that was a want rather than a need?
- Open any bills that arrived via mail or email and schedule a reminder to pay them.
- Check your budget to make sure there is adequate money allocated to cover the bills before they're due.

Here's another habit stack example, related to meals:

- Start dinner. (This could be your trigger, as we'll cover in the next point.)

177   https://www.developgoodhabits.com/building-habit-stacking-routine/

- While dinner is cooking, check your menu to see what you'll cook tomorrow night.

- Review the recipe for tomorrow's dinner and move ingredients from the freezer to the fridge to thaw overnight.

- Check the fridge to see if there are any leftovers you can take to work tomorrow.

- Set the table for tonight's dinner.

- With any remaining time you have (before dinner is ready), start kitchen clean up.

Instead of doing these tasks at random times, we recommend that you schedule them for a specific time of day.

For instance, you may start the dinner habit stack every evening at 6:00 p.m. and start the finance-related habit every evening after you put the kids to bed at 8:00 p.m.

2. Create a habit stacking trigger.

We touched briefly on triggers in step one. We understand that the word "trigger" has different meanings for different people. For our purposes, triggers are essentially reminders that initiate the behavior.

For instance, with the dinner habit stack, the trigger was starting dinner, and with the finance-related habit stack, the trigger was putting the kids to bed.

Here are four ways to use triggers to remind you to start a habit stack:

Triggers should be an existing habit that you do automatically every day, such as brushing your teeth or sitting down at your desk. This matters because you need to be certain you'll never miss a reminder.

Triggers can also be a specific time of day, such as when you wake up, after a meal, or as soon as you get home from work.

Triggers must be easy to complete. Challenging actions, including daily ones, make ineffective triggers because you might occasionally miss a day.

Since it takes a long time to establish a new habit, triggers should be well-established habits that you don't even have to think about. Picking a new habit as a trigger decreases consistency.

3. Identify your common pitfalls.

Perhaps you've tried many money-saving tactics before and failed. To increase the odds of success, it's important to identify your common pitfalls and then design your environment for success.

For example, maybe you've decided that one of the best ways to save money is to eat at home more, but you're currently in the habit of frequently eating out. If that's the case, habits related to menu planning and food prep are crucial. Or maybe you tend to spend more than you make each month, and because of it, you not only go deeper into debt, you also fail to invest in your retirement account. If that describes you, you need to focus on the budgeting habit and automate retirement savings.

Here are some common challenges when it comes to saving money:

- Not wanting friends to think you're cheap
- A spouse that is a spender

- Difficulty resisting "good deals"
- Being too tired to cook when you get home from work
- Having a hard time knowing what meals to prepare
- Friends who like to hang out at the mall or eat at expensive restaurants
- A home with a lot of projects that need to be done
- Pressure to exchange expensive gifts during the holidays
- Spending your entire paycheck as soon as you get paid
- Impulsive buys
- Compulsive credit card use
- Credit card use due to no money for emergencies such as car repairs

4. Design your environment for success.

With money-blowing pitfalls in mind, it's now time to consider how you can design your environment for success so those pitfalls don't derail you. The key is to identify your own pitfalls and then create a plan to avoid giving in to them.

Here are some examples of strategies you can use to design your environment for success:

- Join a meal planning service such as eMeals.[178]
- Do as much food prep as you can ahead of time so that it takes very little time to throw a meal together.
- Keep ingredients on hand for quick and easy meals your family loves. For instance, when Rebecca doesn't feel like

---

178   https://www.developgoodhabits.com/emeals

cooking and yet wants to avoid eating out, she makes quesadillas and fruit or tuna sandwiches with carrot sticks.

- Have a good talk with your family about your need to cut back on holiday and birthday spending.

- Initiate new holiday traditions such as drawing names and purchasing a gift for only one person instead of for the entire extended family.

- Leave your credit cards at home. If you have an extreme problem with credit cards, place them in a can of water that you keep in the freezer so that it's a hassle to use them.

- Prioritize home improvement projects and save up for them.

- Automate your retirement investments so the money for them leaves your account before you have a chance to spend it.

- Implement the 72-hour rule for all non-essential items.

- Have friends over to your place for coffee or dinner. To avoid all of the cost landing on your shoulders, make it potluck style.

- Develop friendships with other frugal people who have similar financial goals.

- Reduce the amount of time you spend with friends and family members who pressure you into spending excessive amounts of money.

- Create a list of free or inexpensive ways to have fun or to pamper yourself.

- Instead of going out to movies with friends, invite them to your place for popcorn and a Netflix or Hulu movie.

- Add free events such as concerts at the library or park to your calendar and attend with your family or friends. To avoid the temptation to shell out money on food vendors, pack a picnic.

- Cancel cable plans that include tempting channels such as shopping networks.

5. Take baby steps along the way.

Start off with habits that are so simple that it's almost impossible to fail.

For example, if you tend to pick up coffee and a pastry on the way to work every day, buy ready-made breakfast treats during your weekly grocery shopping trip. Before bed, set up your coffee pot to have a fresh pot waiting for you when you wake up, then put your pastry into a plastic bag or container so you can grab it and go.

These two simple habits take very little time and yet can save you $100 per month (at a minimum). Small wins like this build emotional momentum because they're easy to remember and take very little time and effort to complete.

The point is that these are such easy tasks to complete that they eliminate the likelihood that you'll skip a day, even if you're tired or stressed. We recommend habits that you can complete in less than five minutes; build your habit stack around those items. Focus on those items for a week or two until that stack is automatic before adding more habits to the routine. Keep adding small habits to your habit-stacking routine until the entire habit stack takes 30 minutes.

6. Reward yourself.

Sticking with your habit-stacking routine is a big deal and deserves a reward. Rewards can motivate you to complete the routine. Your reward can be anything you enjoy, such as watching a TV show or enjoying a cup of your favorite tea. Our only piece of advice is to avoid any rewards that undermine the benefit of your habit.

For example, if you've consistently prepared coffee and bagged up a pastry every night before bed for the past month, don't reward yourself by stopping at Starbucks for a coffee and pastry on the way to work. Splurging on a pound of gourmet coffee beans would be a better reward.

If you need ideas for how to reward yourself, check out Steve's blog post "155 Ways to Reward Yourself for Completing a Goal or Task."[179]

YOUR ACTION PLAN

It's now time to build your first money-saving habit stack. To get started, simply complete the six actions we detailed above.

First, make a list of the habits you'd like to complete every day. Remember that each habit should take less than five minutes, and your entire routine should take less than 30 minutes. Remember that the easier the tasks, the more likely you'll be to turn them into permanent habits.

Next, decide on a trigger for the habit stack. This needs to be a set time of day and will often occur in the same location. Be sure to connect this to something you already do without fail.

179   https://www.developgoodhabits.com/reward-yourself/

Third, identify the money-saving challenges you personally face. For instance, you may be an impulse shopper, have a spouse that is a spender, or not know how to cook. It can be difficult to see your own faults, but we all have them, and your ability to identify yours is a crucial part of your future success.

Next, design your environment to eliminate those challenges. Do this by acknowledging your temptations and coming up with a plan for how to deal with them ahead of time. Don't just think about this. Write down the specific challenges and how you'll avoid them.

Fifth, take baby steps. Start with just a couple of super simple habits that take just a few minutes to complete. Gradually work toward a money-saving habit stack that takes an entire 30 minutes to complete.

Finally, reward yourself for reaching milestones. For instance, give yourself a small treat after sticking with your habit stack for an entire week, a bit bigger reward for sticking with it for two weeks, and a bigger reward for sticking with it for a month. The only caveat is to avoid rewards that undermine your money-saving efforts.

STEP 5: Create Accountability for Your Money-Saving Goals

One of the most important steps to saving money in the long-term is to add *accountability* for every major goal.

Rebecca first learned about the power of accountability through her husband. As a young adult, he struggled with many destructive behaviors, and in spite of his efforts to overcome them, failed. Accountability was the key to creating lasting change. Because of that, shortly after they got married, he introduced the concept of accountability to Rebecca, who also benefitted.

Steve also uses accountability throughout his personal and professional life. He talks every week with another business owner; during these conversations, they share their goals and challenges. He's part of a biweekly mastermind meeting with five other business owners. And when it comes to money, Steve and is wife have frequent conversations about their budget and the way to save for their nest egg.

The bottom line?

A personal commitment alone doesn't work. Big life changes require a solid plan AND a support network. We all need people to cheer us on—or kick us in the butt when we're slacking.

In this chapter we'll cover three accountability strategies.

1. Self-Accountability

As the name implies, this type of accountability is something you do on your own, with the help of a few basic tools. For example, you can use your calender, phone, or sticky notes to remind you to do specific actions.

You can also use habit-tracking apps. We recommend these three in particular:

- StridesApp.com
- Coach.me
- HabitHub[180]

Earlier we mentioned another tool that helps with self-accountability, AmericaSaves.org. Make a finance-related pledge[181] on the site and sign up for emails and text messages to keep your financial goals top-of-mind.

2. In-Person Accountability

In-person accountability is one of the most effective methods of sticking with your habits because it's hard to ignore the friend or family member sitting across from you. The risk of choosing an accountability partner with the same goal as you is that if one of you slips up, it may bring the other one down. For instance, if you and a coworker have decided to eat bagged lunches together every day and one of you shows up without lunch, or even worse suggests a tempting restaurant option, the other may find it hard to resist eating out. To avoid this, have a plan in place for what to do if your buddy falls so you stand strong.

---

180   http://www.thehabithub.com/
181   https://americasaves.org/for-savers/pledge

Instead of a buddy with the same goal, you may choose to be accountable to a spouse, friend, or accountability partner that checks in with you to see how you're doing. If you don't have someone in your personal network to hold you accountable, consider joining a class or even hiring a coach.

3. Online Accountability

Facebook groups are a great way to find like-minded people with similar goals. They are a great place to check in, get advice, and find accountability partners. It's often helpful to join a group that is focused on a particular area of need.

For instance, if you're trying to stick with a budget, search for Facebook groups with a budgeting focus. If consistently cooking meals at home is your biggest money-saving goal, find groups with a focus on easy meal prep. If you want to supercharge your retirement savings so you can retire early, join a Facebook group focused on financial independence. You may need to join a few groups before you find one that's a good fit for you, but don't give up! With just a bit of patience, you're bound to find the group that's right for you.

Here are a few Facebook groups that have an active community:

- ChooseFI[182] was started for the audience of the ChooseFI podcast and blog. Members are encouraged to engage in conversations about financial independence, spending less, investing, and other topics.

- Frugal and FabuLESS[183] is a group focused on how to save

---

182   https://www.facebook.com/groups/ChooseFI/
183   https://www.facebook.com/groups/598937220131710/?fref=ts

on makeup and beauty products so you can be beautiful even on a budget.

- Don't Pay Full—Coupons, Deals and Money Saving Tips![184] discusses all things couponing and offers practical advice on how to save money and spend less. You can ask questions or share tips to help others.

- Families On A Budget (FOAB)[185] is made up of members primarily from the UK. Conversations revolve around couponing, supermarket or online glitches, ideas to make extra money, and making the most out of your food.

- Spend Less Live Better[186] facilitates members helping each other by sharing money-saving tips and bargains.

- Frugal Homemaking Chat Group[187] boasts a group motto: "Use it up, wear it out, make it do or do without!" This group encourages members, mostly moms, to share and ask questions about how to create a wonderful home for families on a budget, money-saving projects, book recommendations, and homemaking crafts.

- Bargain Hunters Tips & Tricks[188] is a great group where you can share your thrift ideas, DIY projects, and bargains and discounts.

---

184   https://www.facebook.com/groups/574907059307427/
185   https://www.facebook.com/groups/574907059307427/
186   https://www.facebook.com/groups/LiveBetterSpendLess/
187   https://www.facebook.com/groups/248600692013250/
188   https://www.facebook.com/groups/276607239189101/

Be Honest about Your Failures

Developing the money-saving habit is a process that evolves over time. It's natural to slip up on occasion. Be honest about your failures, but don't beat yourself up. Just because you fail on occasion doesn't mean that you yourself are a failure, or that you have no hope of finding success.

Keep this in mind when selecting an accountability partner. They are there to support you, not beat you up. So be honest with them as they walk through the financial journey with you.

Never Break the Chain

"Don't break the chain" is a habit-building technique attributed to Jerry Seinfield. As a young comedian, he honed his craft by writing a joke every single day. Every day that he wrote a joke, he marked a red X on the calendar. The more his chain of X's grew, the more motivated he was to write a joke each day so he wouldn't break the chain. Seinfeld's advice is to just keep at it, and your chain will grow longer every single day.

To build your chain, you can use a wall calendar or a habit-tracking app such as Strides,[189] Coach.me, or HabitHub[190] to track your success. To increase the odds of building a long chain, create a mini-habit that takes just a few minutes each day. Even if you spend a few minutes on a money-saving habit, you can consider the day a success.

---

189   https://www.stridesapp.com
190   http://www.thehabithub.com

YOUR ACTION PLAN

Select one of the apps mentioned earlier in this chapter, or purchase a wall calendar to track your primary money-saving daily habit. See how long you can go without breaking the chain!

Next, set up either in-person or online accountability.

Create a milestone such as logging your expenditures every day for 30 days, and then come up with a way to celebrate when you reach the milestone. Be sure that the way you decide to celebrate doesn't conflict with your financial goals.

STEP 6: Do Periodic Reviews

To stay on track and avoid developing deeply ingrained negative habits, plan to review various habits and goals weekly, monthly, quarterly, or annually. Some goals and habits require more frequent or less frequent review.

For instance, Rebecca and her husband spend about 15 minutes every week reviewing and updating their budget, and about an hour each month looking at investments and calculating net worth. Once a year they do a big-picture review of their spending in various categories, rebalancing investment portfolios, and so on.

Regardless of frequency, start your reviews by celebrating both big and small wins. Next, reflect on any mistakes you made, and look for any patterns that got in the way of your financial habits.

As an example, you may realize that you overspend your eat-out budget every Friday, or that your electricity bill doubles every January. Perhaps you'll see that you simply don't have enough budgeted for certain categories, or that you've fallen behind in your retirement savings goals due to a lack of automation or perhaps even due to inadequate income. You might find out that your house costs you more than you realized and that your biggest financial win would require downsizing or relocating.

If you see that the same mistakes keep happening, determine the root cause. Is it because your goals are unrealistic? Are there other obstacles you need to remove?

At the end of each review, ask yourself the following three questions and jot down the answers in your journal:

- What went right?
- What went wrong?
- How can I plan for next week (or month, quarter, or year)?

For example, every week when Rebecca and her husband review their budget, they immediately see if there was any unnecessary spending and make a plan to reduce spending in certain categories to get back on track. Since they review this weekly, things never get too far out of hand. When they do an annual spending review, they can see how much they spend over the course of a year on things like utilities, which makes it easier to know how much, on average, they need to put aside each month.

At the end of your review, devise a plan for overcoming obstacles; if needed, adjust your goals.

YOUR ACTION PLAN

Your first action for this step is to decide exactly what you'll review and when, the questions you'll ask during the reviews, the tools you'll use for the reviews, and what you'll do as a result of the reviews.

For instance, you may review your budget each week using a tool such as You Need a Budget.[191] During your review, ask yourself what did and did not work, and then adapt next week's budget based on what you discovered during the review. During an annual review of your retirement account, you may review your total contribution amount. If your contributions are less than

---

191   https://www.youneedabudget.com/

ideal, make a plan to max them out before the April 15 deadline. You may also see that your portfolio needs to be rebalanced, and as a result of that, move a bit of money around.

One word of caution: don't make this too complicated. If your reviews take too much time, you'll likely struggle to do them consistently.

In light of the above, write the following in your journal:

- What habits or goals you'll review, and how frequently you'll review them
- What questions to ask yourself in the review
- The tools you'll use for your review
- The types of action steps you'll take as a result of the review

Be sure to set a time for your reviews and add them to your calendar. For instance, Rebecca and her husband do their weekly budget review every Saturday morning at 10:00 a.m. The first Saturday of every month, they do their net worth review immediately after their budget meeting. They block out a couple of days to do a deep dive into their finances and review other goals between Christmas and New Year's Day each year.

Be committed to the reviews like you would any other appointment. If something comes up for the same time as the review, instead of skipping the review, schedule it for another time.

STEP 7: Plan for Obstacles

If you read our book, *The Budgeting Habit*,[192] since budgeting and saving money are closely related, some of what we cover in this chapter will be familiar to you, with just a few twists.

The bottom line is that even if you've designed your environment for success, as you work on developing the money-saving habit, you'll encounter obstacles. The best way to overcome obstacles is to anticipate them and have an action plan for dealing with them.

Here are some common money-saving obstacles, along with specific solutions for overcoming them.

Obstacle 1: Unexpected Expenses

Regardless of how much planning you do, and how hard you work on saving money, there will be times when things go wrong. The car breaks down, you get sick and have unexpected medical bills, or you experience some other unexpected financial blow.

There are a couple of ways to handle this, but the easiest way is to consistently add to your emergency fund so that you always have money set aside for the unexpected. Secondly, keep regular expenses such as quarterly or annual car insurance payments on your radar, and add to these funds on a regular basis.

---

192   https://www.amazon.com/Budgeting-Habit-Budget-Develop-Habits
-ebook/dp/B07F8J6DKP

Obstacle 2: Impulse Buys

We've also discussed the dangers of the impulse buy habit. But in addition to that, here are a few more strategies that might help:

- Use the cash envelope system for everything other than regular monthly bills. When the money runs out, stop spending.

- Use a shopping list and commit to sticking to it. If it's not on the list, put it down and walk away.

- Unsubscribe from email lists that pitch tempting products or services.

- Avoid shopping channels or network television with commercials.

- To keep from feeling deprived, rather than telling yourself, "I can't buy it" say, "I'll buy it tomorrow."

- Leave your credit cards at home. Even better, freeze your credit cards in a coffee can filled with water so that it takes time and effort to access them.

- Avoid shopping with friends that are big spenders.

Obstacle 3: Friends and Family

Friends and family, including spouses, often form the biggest obstacle to saving money. This is a sensitive area because especially when it comes to family, most likely, you want to continue the relationship with them. The key is to communicate with them—more than once if needed!

If your spouse is a spender and you're a saver, take the time to talk through your goals. Listen and make concessions where needed.

For instance, if your spouse has an expensive hobby, rather than trying to get them to give it up completely, see if they're willing to reduce the amount they spend. For example, if they golf every week, see if they'd be willing to cut back to once or twice a month. If they like to eat out, and you like to cook, offer to make some of their favorite meals at home.

Friends are easier to deal with than spouses because you likely don't have shared finances. Suggest less expensive activities, and host fun and inexpensive activities in your home such as a Netflix movie and popcorn instead of going out. If you have friends that consistently pressure you to spend money, reduce the amount of time you spend with them, and work on developing friendships with more budget-conscious friends.

Obstacle 4: Inadequate Income

The great news is, many of the strategies in this book will help you have a decent lifestyle, even if you have a relatively low income. But other things, such as maxing out retirement accounts, are difficult to do on a low income, even if you live frugally. There's really only two ways to deal with this, and that is to make more money, or else drastically reduce your living expenses through things like geo arbitrage or going carless.

While finding a higher-paying job may be an option, consider working a side hustle to bring in more income.

Obstacle 5: Eating Out

For Rebecca and her husband, eating out is always the bigger source of temptation since it's something they've done from the very beginning of their 30+ years of marriage. It's hard to break that temptation, but so worth it since it's much cheaper to eat at home.

Meal planning and having a routine for shopping and food prep is the primary way to overcome this obstacle. It also helps to have freezer meals and other easy-to-prepare foods on hand. Rebecca likes to make her own homemade convenience foods such as homemade frozen pizza and taco kits for those days when they're in the mood for a restaurant meal. They've also had good results with Takeout Kit[193] since they are shelf-stable and focus on restaurant-style ethnic food.

When You Mess Up ...

No matter how hard you try, there may be times when you mess up. Perhaps you fail to contribute as much to your retirement account as you promised you would, or you succumb to the temptation to use your credit card, or you blow money on an expensive outfit.

In spite of the discouragement and perhaps guilt you feel when this type of thing happens, don't give up! Take a moment to revisit your purpose for saving money so you'll remember why it matters so much.

Yes, you do need to be honest with yourself, but you don't need to beat yourself up when you fail. Every day is a new day and provides an opportunity for a fresh start.

---

193   https://takeoutkit.com/

YOUR ACTION PLAN

First, grab your journal and write about which of the obstacles above hit close to home.

Next, using our examples as inspiration, write down a list of tactics you can use to overcome these obstacles. For example, if you find yourself going back into debt again and again, you may choose to get rid of all credit cards, or if you're not quite ready for that, freeze them in a can of water. If people close to you are your primary obstacle, schedule a time to talk with them about the financial changes you need to make. Be sure to do it when you're in a calm and non-judgmental state of mind.

If you need to increase your income in order to meet your financial goals, consider whether you need to make a job change or if starting a side hustle is a better option. If you need to make a job change, update your resume and schedule a bit of time each week to scour online job searching sites.

As always, don't make too many drastic changes at once. Commit to one or two actions that address your current biggest obstacle.

STEP 8: Maximize Those "Slivers of Time"

Even if you only have a few minutes to work on saving money, we recommend that you still do something. The idea here is to use those "short slivers of time."

Suzanne Perez Tobias recommends that in addition to any daily habits you develop, you can also maximize short slivers of time[194] to make steady progress with your goals. It's true that spending five minutes on a money-saving task may not seem to have a huge impact, but when done consistently, those little bits of time add up.

Here are some examples of how to use short slivers of time to save money:

- Write down expenditures as they occur.
- Check the weekly grocery store sales flyers and add any deals to your shopping list.
- Clip coupons while watching TV.
- Check your bank balance or your budget app on your phone before making a purchase.
- Add the Amazon Kindle app and load it up with personal finance books to read whenever you have a few spare minutes.
- Divide leftovers into single-serving containers for grab-and-go lunches.
- Review your goals and make sure your actions move you closer to your desired outcomes.

---

194   http://articles.chicagotribune.com/2007-05-27/features/0705230443_1_f ree-time-picture-frames-minutes

- Check all your financial statements to make sure there are no unauthorized charges.
- Check your cell phone data usage to make sure you won't exceed your limits.

Spare moments of time that you have throughout the day may seem insignificant, but if you commit to using those small slivers of time effectively, they'll have a big impact on your financial bottom line.

YOUR ACTION PLAN

During the next week, make a point of being mindful of wasted bits of time and jot them down. (If you think you'll have a hard time remembering to do this, set a reminder on your phone. When the reminder goes off, take a moment to think about how you may have wasted time over the past few hours.) Also, think about the recurring things that happen each week such as waiting to pick up your child from school, or waiting for friends or family members to show up for an activity.

The point of this exercise is to first see how much time you do have that can be used productively. This is especially helpful if you feel that you just don't have time to devote to saving money! The more you do this, the more you'll tune in to those little slivers of time so that you'll be less likely to waste them.

Challenge yourself to come up with a list of at least ten little bits of free time that occurred in a single week. Divide that list into things that happen regularly versus infrequently. For instance, you may wait for your kids to finish getting ready for school every morning, but you only wait to be seen at the doctor's office or bank a few times a year.

Once you have your two lists, create a list of statements for how you'll use those slivers of time. For instance, "When I'm waiting for the oven to preheat, I'll pack tomorrow's lunch," or "When I'm waiting at the doctor's office, I'll check my bank account and update my budget."

STEP 9: 7 Ways to Scale Up Your Money-Saving Efforts

If you want to supercharge your progress toward your financial goals, you can scale up with personal challenges. We shared some of these challenges in our book, *The Budgeting Habit*,[195] and are repeating them here as a reminder, or in case you haven't yet read that book. We're also sharing two new bonus ideas.

Here are seven ideas to get you started.

1. Establish a temporary spending freeze. A *spending freeze* is simply a decision to not spend money in a specific category or in all categories for a set period of time. For instance, if you typically spend a lot of money eating out or picking up coffee on the way to work, make a commitment not to do that for a week, month, or longer. Some people go beyond this and spend money only on essentials such as paying rent or their mortgage payment, utilities, and groceries for an entire year.

Regardless of what type of spending freeze you choose, apply all of the money you save toward a goal such as paying off debt or maxing out your retirement account.

2. Gradually decrease spending. If a spending freeze seems too extreme, work toward gradually decreasing your spending in a specific category. For this option, it makes the most sense to choose a category that you currently spend a lot of money on and that is somewhat flexible. For example, this wouldn't work on something like rent or house payment since, while they are high-cost, they're fixed amounts without any wiggle room.

---

195 https://www.amazon.com/Budgeting-Habit-Budget-Develop-Habits-ebook/dp/B07F8J6DKP

However, groceries or eating out work since food is costly and often includes a lot of discretionary spending.

To gradually decrease your spending, look at how much you've spent on average over the last few months, and challenge yourself to spend a bit less each month over the next few months or year. For instance, if you currently spend $1,000 per month on groceries, try spending $900 this month, $800 next month, and so on. Do this until you hit a point where you feel stretched but not frustrated.

3. Gradually increase savings or investing. If you feel that you can't afford to put money into your savings or investment accounts, or if you put only very little into those accounts, gradually increase the amounts. For instance, if you currently put nothing into savings or retirement accounts, start with a super small level such as $5 per week. After a month of doing this, increase it to $6 per week, and after that $7, and so on. This challenge goes hand in hand with the previous two challenges because as you save money in various areas, you'll have extra money to invest.

To make this challenge even easier, invest the money as soon as you're paid. Assuming that you take baby steps with increasing this amount and stop when it hits the point of being too much, you'll find that you manage to live on what's left after paying yourself first.

4. Embark on an income-producing challenge. Sometimes bringing in more income is the best way to increase your retirement or other savings accounts or to pay off debt. You can do this by taking on an additional part-time job, or by starting a side hustle. If you're unfamiliar with the side hustle concept, or if you need ideas, be sure to check out Nick Loper's blog post

"99 Side Hustle Business Ideas You Can Start Today"[196] and his book, *Buy Buttons*.[197] Both provide a great overview of different income-generating opportunities and what you need to do to create a similar business.

5. Make a game of it. Here are two financial games you can play if you struggle with impulse spending.

Double or Nothing

Start by picking an unnecessary spending category that you want to cut back on, such as eating out. Next, pick something you want to put more money into, such as a retirement account or paying off debt.

Next, for a set period of time—such as a week, month, or 90 days—put the same amount of money that you spend on the unnecessary category into your savings or retirement account.

For instance, if you go out to dinner and spend $50, you also have to put $50 into your savings or retirement account. Since that dinner ends up costing $100, you may think twice about spending the money. Even if you do spend the money, half of it moves you closer to one of your financial goals, so it's a win either way.

Do This Not That

This game helps you find less expensive alternatives.

For instance, instead of ordering a pizza, make a simple meal at home. Instead of buying a new outfit at the mall, head to the thrift store and see if you can find something similar at a much

---

196   https://www.sidehustlenation.com/ideas/
197   http://www.developgoodhabits.com/buy-buttons

lower price. You can also apply this to other purchases such as new furniture or appliances by buying a used, or new but less expensive, alternative.

After choosing the less-expensive alternative, calculate how much you saved and apply that amount to paying off debt or to one of your other financial goals.

6. Increase automated investments into your IRA. One of the best ways to max out your IRA account is to automate the process. For instance, in 2019, the maximum amount you can contribute is $6,000, or $7,000 if you're age 50 and over. The best way to make sure you max out your account is to calculate how this breaks down monthly and then automate those contributions. For instance, $6,000 divided by 12 is $500 per month, and $7,000 divided by 12 is $583.33 per month.

To supercharge the amount you contribute to your investments, instead of taking 12 months to do this, do it in ten. For those under the age of 50, that would be $600 per month instead of $500, and for those 50+, that would be $700 per month instead of $583.33.

Once you've maxed out your IRA contributions in ten months, for the remaining two months of the year, send the money you're already used to paying into a non-retirement account such as a savings account, regular investment account, or an education or custodial account for your children.

7. Gradually increase the percent of your income you invest. Another way to increase the amount you invest is to gradually increase the percentage you invest. For instance, if you currently invest 10% of your income to your retirement account, up that to 11%, and then a few months later to 12%, and so on.

YOUR ACTION PLAN

Pick one challenge to start on within the next 48 hours. For example, if a spending freeze sounds like an option, determine the specific item you won't buy, and how long the spending freeze will last. If you need to bring in extra income, read Nick Loper's blog post linked to in #4 above, and make a list of three to five ideas to explore in more detail.

Over the next three months, see how much extra money you can save, or how much additional money you can bring in through a side hustle, and then apply that money to one of your big financial goals.

Now Is the Time ...

Congratulations, you've reached the end of the book!

Hopefully, by now you've bookmarked, highlighted, or taken notes on a few strategies you can use to immediately save money.

So what should you do now?

Well, we suggest that you complete three immediate actions as soon as you finish this section:

1. Pick One Area of Focus

What's the best way to get started with the stack your savings habit?

Simple:

Pick your biggest "problem area" and get to work.

Yes, we know this is an oversimplification, but the real secret to gaining value from any book is to start *somewhere*. Your somewhere will be different from others. But we suggest that you identify that one area that keeps you up at night and attack it with all you've got.

Drowning in debt?

Then use one of the three debt reduction strategies we mentioned in Lever 1.

Wasting money on expensive dinner and takeout meals?

Then incorporate the meal planning habit into your busy schedule.

Confused about why you have nothing left after every paycheck?

Then analyze your bills and plug up those spending leaks!

Yes, you probably have dozens of ideas that you want to implement, but the biggest result you can get right now is to identify your biggest challenges and work through them in a systematic, step-by-step manner.

2. Commit to the Stack Your Savings Process

Saving money isn't a one-time action—it requires a lifelong commitment. Moreover, there *will* be times when you slip up. In fact, both Rebecca and Steve still make the occasional mistake with their finances. But when they do slip up, they learn from the experience and make sure it never happens again.

In the previous section, we included a nine-step framework to build great financial habits. *Our advice?* Review this section immediately and then take action.

And if you're unsure about what to do first? Then just pick *anything* and get started. Honestly, there is no such thing as a "perfect plan." Instead, you can build perfection in your life by discovering new ideas, making mistakes, and learning from each experience.

3. Journal about Your Experiences

One way to master your finances is to keep an ongoing journal of your experiences. This is important for three reasons. First, you'll develop personal accountability because you'll have to "check in" daily and log your financial decisions. This will subconsciously help you make better financial decisions. Next, writing about your challenges (and wins) provides an emotional outlet that allows you to be perfectly candid about your financial journey. Finally, this journal will become a time capsule you can review in the future. One day you'll look back and be amazed at how much you've grown.

Now, when we say "journal," that doesn't mean you have to buy a physical book (but we do feel it's the best option). In fact, you have a couple of options here:

- A blank physical journal (Steve uses the Essentials Dot Matrix Notebook[198])
- A software program like You Need a Budget (YNAB)[199]
- A spreadsheet program like Excel[200] or Google Sheets[201]
- A blog or a website
- A Facebook group or other public forum

Really, the journaling tool you pick is irrelevant. What's important is to develop the habit of checking in daily and writing down your experiences. For more on this, we recommend checking out the book *Effortless Journaling*[202] that Steve co-authored with Barrie Davenport.

Okay, you now have your marching orders, so let's get started with the three suggestions that we just outlined.

Before you go, we want to remind you that saving money is a long journey. Your first steps aren't that important. What *is*

198   https://www.developgoodhabits.com/essentials-matrix-journal
199   https://www.developgoodhabits.com/youneedabudget
200   https://office.live.com/start/Excel.aspx
201   https://www.google.com/sheets/about/
202   https://www.developgoodhabits.com/effortless-journaling

important is making the commitment to *daily* action. You might struggle in the beginning. But eventually you will reach a point where you'll be able to put less money toward bills and more money toward your important short- and long-term goals.

We wish you the best of luck on the *stack your savings* journey!

Cheers,

S.J. Scott & Rebecca Livermore

Thank You!

Before you go, we'd like to say thank you for purchasing our book.

You could have picked from dozens of books on habit development, but you took a chance and checked out this one.

So, big thanks for purchasing this book and reading all the way to the end.

Now we'd like to ask for a small favor. **Could you please take a minute or two and leave a review for this book on Amazon?**

This feedback will help us continue to write the kind of books that help you get results. And if you loved it, please let us know.

More Books by Steve

How to Stop Procrastinating: A Simple Guide to Mastering Difficult Tasks and Breaking the Procrastination Habit

10-Minute Mindfulness: 71 Habits for Living in the Present Moment

Habit Stacking: 127 Small Actions to Improve Your Health, Wealth, and Happiness

Novice to Expert: 6 Steps to Learn Anything, Increase Your Knowledge, and Master New Skills

Declutter Your Mind: How to Stop Worrying, Relieve Anxiety, and Eliminate Negative Thinking

The Miracle Morning for Writers: How to Build a Writing Ritual That Increases Your Impact and Your Income

10-Minute Digital Declutter: The Simple Habit to Eliminate Technology Overload

10-Minute Declutter: The Stress-Free Habit for Simplifying Your Home

The Accountability Manifesto: How Accountability Helps You Stick to Goals

Confident You: An Introvert's Guide to Success in Life and Business

Exercise Every Day: 32 Tactics for Building the Exercise Habit (Even If You Hate Working Out)

The Daily Entrepreneur: 33 Success Habits for Small Business Owners, Freelancers and Aspiring 9-to-5 Escape Artists

Master Evernote: The Unofficial Guide to Organizing Your Life with Evernote (Plus 75 Ideas for Getting Started)

Bad Habits No More: 25 Steps to Break Any Bad Habit

Habit Stacking: 97 Small Life Changes That Take Five Minutes or Less

To-Do List Makeover: A Simple Guide to Getting the Important Things Done

23 Anti-Procrastination Habits: How to Stop Being Lazy and Overcome Your Procrastination

S.M.A.R.T. Goals Made Simple: 10 Steps to Master Your Personal and Career Goals

115 Productivity Apps to Maximize Your Time: Apps for iPhone, iPad, Android, Kindle Fire and PC/iOS Desktop Computers

Writing Habit Mastery: How to Write 2,000 Words a Day and Forever Cure Writer's Block

Daily Inbox Zero: 9 Proven Steps to Eliminate Email Overload

Wake Up Successful: How to Increase Your Energy and Achieve Any Goal with a Morning Routine

10,000 Steps Blueprint: The Daily Walking Habit for Healthy Weight Loss and Lifelong Fitness

70 Healthy Habits: How to Eat Better, Feel Great, Get More Energy and Live a Healthy Lifestyle

Resolutions That Stick! How 12 Habits Can Transform Your New Year

More Books by Rebecca

Blogging

Blogger's Quick Guide to Starting Your First WordPress Blog

Blogger's Quick Guide to Writing Rituals and Routines

Blogger's Quick Guide to Blog Post Ideas

Blogger's Quick Guide to Working with a Team

Blogging for Authors

Content Repurposing Made Easy

Christian Living

Godly Freedom: Devotional Readings from 1 Corinthians

By the Will of God: Christian Devotional Readings from 2 Corinthians

Faith that Forgives: Christian Devotional Readings from Philemon

A Fresh Start with Jesus: Embracing the God of Second Chances

India Travel

Rickshaws, Rajas and Roti

Co-Written with Steve Scott

The Daily Entrepreneur

Level Up Your Day

Confident You

The Budgeting Habit